The Limits of Mortality

An Essay on Wordsworth's Major Poems

The LIMITS of MORTALITY

An Essay on Wordsworth's Major Poems

by DAVID FERRY

Wesleyan University Press

MIDDLETOWN, CONNECTICUT

This book is lovingly dedicated

to my parents

Contents

Preface

THE TRADITION of scholarship out of which I am working might be described as a reaction against the "Arnoldian" tendency to take Wordsworth's vocabulary of feeling at face value, saying that he gave us back the simplicity and force of our emotions, which neoclassicism was supposed somehow to have taken away; also as a reaction against attempts, like that of Sir Leslie Stephen, to endow Wordsworth with a coherent morality or ethic and to define him primarily in moral or ethical terms. The writers with whom this book has most in common have all tended to define Wordsworth in metaphysical terms, as a geographer of the relation of man and nature, of nature and eternity, of man and eternity; and therefore they have tended to see his language not as an exercise in "simplicity" and "naturalness" but as a symbolic system. Often these interests are more or less implicit in such writers, but the tendency is plain. I came to all my major conclusions about Wordsworth's poetry before I had read these writers, and indeed I found myself in some disagreement with all of them in one way or another; but I wish to acknowledge the confidence they have given me that there was at least *some* truth in what I was saying.

I am especially indebted to G. Wilson Knight's brilliant essay called "The Wordsworthian Profundity," in *The Starlit Dome* (Oxford, 1940); D. G. James' book *Scepticism and Poetry* (London, 1937); Geoffrey H. Hartman's *The Unmediated Vision* (New Haven, 1954): and three articles, James R. Baird's "Wordsworth's 'Inscrutable Workmanship' and the Emblems of Conduct" (*PMLA*, LXVIII, 444–457); Walter Jackson Bate's "Coleridge on the Function of Art," in *Perspectives of Criticism* (ed. Harry Levin, Cambridge, Massachusetts, 1950); and Morse Peckham's

"Toward a Theory of Romanticism" (*PMLA*, LXVI, 5–23). The similarities between my argument and theirs at various points will be obvious to the reader, and so will the differences, which need not be argued here. I wish to recommend also two recent books as, perhaps, counterirritants to my own, F. W. Bateson's *Wordsworth: A Re-Interpretation* (London, 1954) and John Jones' *The Egotistical Sublime: A History of Wordsworth's Imagination* (London, 1954). In a more general way, I wish to acknowledge the help in finding my way that was provided by Basil Willey's *The Seventeenth Century Background* (London, 1934) —the chapter on Wordsworth and Locke—and Alfred North Whitehead's *Science and the Modern World* (New York, 1925). I have also been immensely helped in this sense by Professor Bate's *From Classic to Romantic* (Cambridge, Massachusetts, 1946). Various other books and articles have been useful to me, but none, I think, in a sufficiently direct way to require acknowledgment.

I am extremely grateful for the help, advice, and encouragement of a number of teachers, colleagues, and friends—Professors W. J. Bate, Douglas Bush, and Reuben Brower, Dr. Richard Poirier, and my wife, Dr. Anne Davidson Ferry, of Harvard University; Professor Thomas R. Edwards, of the University of California; and Professors Walter E. Houghton, Ruth Michael, Virginia Prettyman, and Robert E. Garis, of Wellesley College. Professors Bate, Bush, and Garis, and my wife, have been especially generous with their time and patience in reading this manuscript at various stages of its writing. And I am intellectually indebted to Professor Brower in more ways than I can count.

I am depending faithfully on the reader's interest in the close reading of whole poems here, and my argument proceeds in terms of such readings. That is to say, I have interested myself not only in prosecuting a general argument about this poetry but also in the close reading of many of the best poems of Wordsworth's major period, for their own sakes.

To avoid distracting the reader unduly, I have given line references only to *The Prelude*, and to reduce the number of references there, my citations are occasionally not simply to the passage quoted directly but to the longer passage under discussion, of which the direct quotation is part. In the first three chapters the shorter poems are almost always quoted in full, and where they are not I think the location of lines under discussion is always plain.

For purposes of economy I have paid no attention to *The Excursion*, not even to those parts which were written during the period under consideration here. The reader can decide for himself whether or not what I say here applies there. I think it does. I have also neglected the long and to me very impressive poem *Peter Bell*, also for purposes of economy. For somewhat different reasons I have not paid attention to many of the sonnets, even of this period (roughly 1798–1805), since they represent, I think, a somewhat different Wordsworth, who might well be the subject of another book.

Some of the notions expressed in this book appear, in a very summary form, in my introduction to the *Laurel Wordsworth* (Dell Books, 1959).

The Limits of Mortality

An Essay on Wordsworth's Major Poems

Some Characteristics of
Wordsworth's Style

THE CHAPTERS which follow this one are an attempt to define the subject matter which occupied the central place in William Wordsworth's imagination during his major creative period (which I think of as extending roughly from 1798 to 1805), and an attempt, furthermore, to relate this central preoccupation to various other important aspects of his work. My argument proceeds by a series of readings—as painstaking and detailed as seems necessary—of some of the most interesting poems of that period, and it seeks to develop through those readings a consistent and sufficiently complex view of the poet's mind in operation.

It is the main function of the critic of any poet to discover in him ideas and feelings which can in some way be related to our own deepest feelings and ideas, and which are able to make their appeal ultimately outside the limits of their own time. These are the truly formative contents of any good poem, since all its other evidences of unity proceed from them and since all its other, lesser meanings must subsist in them or else be considered irrelevant. Thus, if one should decide that *Lycidas* is merely a poem about the death of Edward King, or merely about the social and spiritual condition of England in Milton's time, then two conclusions are possible—*Lycidas* is minor, or else the critic has not gone far enough to discover its truly formative subject matter, by which alone the poem can be finally judged. Wordsworth says:

> Aristotle, I have been told, has said, that Poetry is the most philosophic of all writing: it is so: its object is truth, not individual and local, but general and operative; not standing upon external testimony, but carried alive into the heart by passion; truth which is its own testimony, which gives competence and confidence to the tribunal to which it appeals, and receives them from the same tribunal.[1]

This kind of truth, as it exists in poetry, is what the critic has to find, and he will know it when he has found it, because it will be its own testimony that he has done so. This kind of truth, I believe, can be found along the line where the critic's insights into content and his insights into style join and become one.

My general conclusion, after an attempt to perform this critical function, is that the ideas and feelings in Wordsworth's best poems are indeed "in some way" related to the ideas and feelings we are accustomed to find in a more humane poetry, but related as a great enemy, say, is related to a great hero—as an enemy almost equal in strength to that hero, and loving him almost, but an enemy nevertheless. The ideas and feelings in Wordsworth's most important poems are lovingly hostile to the humane world. I shall try to show how this is true by concentrating on one central subject matter: man's relations to nature with respect to his mortality. For it is the limits of mortality that define man as what he is, individual, idiosyncratic, circumscribed; and it is against the mortal limitations of man that Wordsworth, in my view of him, conceived such a hatred.

To say the very least, this is not the usual view of Wordsworth. That is why I have chosen for the most part to develop my argument through the patient reading of whole poems, rather than more generally and topically and by the quotation of selected passages merely. My case can be argued most effectively by demonstrating how such meanings emerge from their fullest poetic context.

My view of Wordsworth derives from a special way of reading his poems—a way of reading which of course I think is the right one. A poet's style is in the last analysis the habit of reading he trains us in—Wordsworth himself said that an original poet must create "the taste by which he is relished." But Wordsworth has often in the past been read without regard to the special sorts of demands the poems make on us, and this resistance to his training has led to a good deal of distortion. In this introductory chapter, therefore, I shall try to define some of the special qualities of Wordsworth's style and consequently to describe the habits of reading with which I have read him.

For this purpose it is useful to examine some criticisms Coleridge made of Wordsworth, because in them Coleridge himself

(surprisingly enough) demonstrates how the poetry can be mis-
understood if it is read with the wrong assumptions in mind. Coleridge, to be sure, thought the criticisms trifling and minor, but I
think we will be able to see that their implications are very far
from being so.

In the *Biographia Literaria*, Coleridge cites as one of Wordsworth's characteristic defects that of employing "thoughts and
images too great for the subject." This, he says,

> . . . is an approximation to what might be called *mental* bombast,
> as distinguished from verbal: for, as in the latter there is a dispro-
> portion of the expressions to the thoughts, so in this there is a dis-
> proportion of thought to the circumstances and occasion.

One of his examples of this fault is the poem *Gipsies*, in which

> . . . the poet, having gone out for a day's tour of pleasure, meets
> early in the morning with a knot of *gipsies*, who had pitched their
> blanket-tents and straw-beds, together with their children and asses,
> in some field by the road-side. At the close of day on his return our
> tourist found them in the same place. "Twelve hours," says he,

> > "Twelve hours, twelve bounteous hours are gone, while I
> > Have been a traveller under open sky,
> > Much witnessing of change and cheer,
> > Yet as I left I find them here."

> Whereat the poet, without seeming to reflect that the poor tawny
> wanderers might probably have been tramping for weeks together
> through road and lane, over moor and mountain, and consequently
> must have been right glad to rest themselves, their children and
> cattle for one whole day; and overlooking the obvious truth, that
> such repose might be quite as necessary for *them*, as a walk of the
> same continuance was pleasing or healthful for the more fortunate
> poet; expresses his indignation in a series of lines, the diction and
> imagery of which would have been rather above, than below the
> mark, had they been applied to the immense empire of China im-
> progressive for thirty centuries:

> > "The weary SUN betook himself to rest:—
> > Outshining, like a visible God,
> > The glorious path, in which he trod!

And now, ascending, after one dark hour,
And one night's diminution of her power,
Behold the mighty MOON! this way
She looks, as if at them—but they
Regard not her:—oh better wrong and strife,
Better vain deeds or evil than such life!
The silent HEAVENS have goings on:
The STARS have tasks!—but *these* have none!" ²

This passage calls on us to judge the verses by the touchstone
of our most humane and sympathetic reactions to things. For
Coleridge the main point is the actual condition of the gipsies
themselves, and in order to judge the poem he draws on his own
knowledge, as a human being aware of the fortunes of other human beings, of how tired and how glad to rest the gipsies must
often be. He accuses the poet of having overlooked an obvious
truth about these "poor tawny wanderers" which he should not
have overlooked, of having in his own good fortune lorded it over
creatures less fortunate than himself. Furthermore, he says that
the diction and imagery expended on these objects are too ele-
vated and would have been so even if they had been expended
on something far more imposing, say the immense torpid empire
of China.

The common-sense foundation of this criticism, the confidence
that the gipsies should be "placed" properly in relation to the
world around them, might in a very simple way be called "classicist": the poet's function is to be a more or less disinterested but
always humane observer of the world outside himself, whose objects have inherent values from which the poet draws the conclusions which propel and direct his sympathies and antipathies.
He looks out on the world, and because his awareness of the
human condition is large and sympathetic, he misses no obvious
truths which call for his pity and tolerance. But at the same time
he is able to see things within the grander frame or structure of
values which obtains in the world, and so is never impelled to use
impertinent or grandiose language about things whose claims are
humble. To such a poet, every object is the meeting ground of
two noncontradictory systems of values, those they contain "within
themselves" and those they have within the total scheme. It is the

poet's duty and special privilege to know both kinds of values and to express their coming together in his language.)

Judged by such criteria, it is plain enough that the poem is silly and intolerant, full of a propertied self-content. Gipsies do obviously get tired and need to rest; to cavil at them for it seems mere uninteresting peevishness. And the reader is after all likely to be both puzzled and irritated when the poet calls on sun, moon, and stars to support his caviling. It is shooting a mouse with an elephant gun.

But perhaps such criteria do not really apply. Perhaps it is of the nature of this imagination to overlook "obvious truths" and to treat a band of gipsies like the empire of China. Wordsworth says that the poet is a man "pleased with his own passions and volitions as manifested in the goings-on of the Universe, and habitually impelled to create them where he does not find them." [3] His tenderness is to be lavished on these passions and volitions, not on the outside world, and whatever attention he pays to that world is in the search for versions of those passions and volitions in other things. If the search should fail, the poet is even compelled to make it a success by creating them where he does not find them. Where Coleridge asserts that the poet has obligations to the actual circumstances and conditions of what he sees, that the poet is bound to a sane and just response to what is true of them "in themselves," Wordsworth asserts an extraordinary freedom for the poet from such obligations, the freedom to ignore whatever is irrelevant to his sublime egotism. It is a freedom which upsets the hierarchical system of values within which the empire of China is thought more than a band of gipsies, and which radically alters the way the poet will regard the band of gipsies in itself. The difference is the difference between a poetry which *evaluates* the world according to a reasonable and common-sense set of attitudes, and a poetry which *makes use of* the world for other purposes.

We are misled if we understand by "passions and volitions" simply the ordinary complex and multifoliate responses and desires of most men's inner lives. Wordsworth's passions and volitions are specifically religious and metaphysical, and their nature is such as to obliterate all others insofar as possible. Spinoza, whose mind in this respect was very similar to Wordsworth's, provides us with a useful vocabulary here. He says:

From all this we easily conceive what is the power which clear and distinct knowledge, and especially that . . . kind of knowledge . . . whose foundation is the knowledge itself of God, possesses over the affects; the power, namely, by which it is able, in so far as they are passions, if not actually to destroy them . . . , at least to make them constitute the smallest part of the mind. . . . Moreover, it begets a love towards an immutable and eternal object . . . , of which we are really partakers . . . ; a love which therefore cannot be vitiated by the defects which are in common love, but which can always become greater and greater . . . occupy the largest part of the mind . . . , and thoroughly affect it.[4]

He also says:

Everything which the mind understands under the form of eternity, it understands not because it conceives the present actual existence of the body, but because it conceives the essence of the body under the form of eternity.[5]

And he explains this further by saying:

Things are conceived by us as actual in two ways: either in so far as we conceive them to exist with relation to a fixed time and place, or in so far as we conceive them to be contained in God, and to follow from the necessity of the divine nature. But those things which are conceived in this second way as true or real we conceive under the form of eternity, and their ideas involve the eternal and infinite essence of God.[6]

Coleridge's criticism of Wordsworth essentially means, then, that the poet failed to take sufficient account of the gipsies conceived as existing "with relation to a fixed time and place." But if we think of the poet as interested in his own passions and volitions "as manifested in the goings-on of the Universe"—that is, as "contained within God"—we see that he has the authority of Spinoza for reducing to "the smallest part of the mind," for destroying as far as possible, that "common love" which might have seen that the gipsies were tired.

Indeed, Wordsworth would be true to himself if he were to blame the gipsies precisely *because* they are tired, for their weariness is the symptom of their condition with relation to a fixed

time and place, the symptom of a stubborn particularity which
resists and denies the eternal. Wordsworth blames the gipsies for
their mortality, for not participating sufficiently in the eternal.
He himself participates by imitating the immense courteous interchanges of sun, moon, and stars, emblems of the eternal nature
of things, and the tone he takes toward the gipsies is to be thought
of not as some glum trivial irritability, but as a sublime arrogance
which is almost identified with his joy in the processes of the universe and takes its justification from that joy. And the magnificent
imagery with which he bombards the gipsies is not inappropriate,
since he is judging them "under the form of eternity" and by
contrast to the mighty creatures of the cosmos, sun, moon, and
stars. In the freedom of his sublime egotism, the gipsies are a
mere convenience for the poet, to express his feelings about eternity. And for this he sacrifices the humane and common-sense
considerations which Coleridge has to take into account.

Coleridge also criticized a more famous poem, *I wandered
lonely as a cloud*, as exhibiting this same "defect" of "thoughts
and images too great for the subject." This poem presents a more
intricate problem.

Here again, Coleridge read the poem as if the poet were looking at the daffodils "with relation to a fixed time and place," and
of course from one point of view we do respond to it in that way.
Coleridge thought Wordsworth had an experience of a particular
event, "a vivid image or visual spectrum," and that he had an
excessive response to that experience. Daffodils are really too
trivial for the attentions of the "inward eye," which might better
be reserved for a moral experience of a much higher order, "the
joy of retrospection, when the images and virtuous actions of a
whole well-spent life, pass before that conscience which is indeed
'the bliss of solitude.'" [7] Even if we grant his assumptions in this
case, we do not go along with his strictures quite as readily in this
poem as in *Gipsies*. We are all familiar with the pleasures a pretty
scene can afford, and the scene of daffodils by a lake is a very
pretty one indeed. And we are willing to admit that there are con-
siderable emotional possibilities in such a scene, whose effects are
ultimately therapeutic. So Coleridge's demand for a more profound
and moral subject matter may perhaps seem captious, too solemn
for the charming occasion. But on further reflection there *does*

seem to be something more here than the occasion warrants, something which Coleridge's moral vocabulary of "conscience" and of
a "well-spent life" cannot tell us much about.

Under the aspect of eternity, daffodils, in their joyous organization, in their dancing, represent as well as anything else the
divine organization of things, the "goings-on of the Universe."
And it is even a rhetorical advantage to the poet that daffodils,
such mere pretty flowers, so humble and modest in the great
scheme of things, can represent such grandeur. In the beginning
the poet is what the gipsies were, emblem of that which does not
participate in the eternal. But in his case, by a process of abstraction, by removing himself from the actual scene, and by a process
of imagination, by seeing what the daffodils mean as "contained
in God," he is able at last to join them, to perceive in them those
passions and volitions which in his loneliness he had temporarily
lost. And his loneliness has nothing to do with a separation from
the world of men. It is a separation from the harmony of things
and the aspect of eternity. The whole action of the poem is the
symbol of the poet's relation to eternity (and the difficulty of per-
fecting that relation), of which his experience of daffodils is merely
an example.

Certain "obvious truths" about a band of gipsies are ignored
in order that they may be used as part of a symbolic design that
figures forth the relations of the poet's mind to the universe; a
degree of emotion is invested in a field of daffodils which seems
excessive if we consider them "with relation to a fixed time and
place." The Romantic metaphysical poet of this sort is likely to
view nature, then, not as a set of objects, events, conditions which
are in themselves his final interest, his final subject matter,
but as a *language to be read,* signposts to that metaphysical place
to which he wants to go. Insofar as those signposts appear to give
him right directions, he will celebrate them, they will seem to him
to be holy. And what the objects of physical nature are to the
metaphysical nature of which he wants to have experience, the
"surface" of his poems—its imagery and its feelings as expressed
in tone and attitude—are to its "deeper meanings," its ultimate
subject matter, which is the celebration of the metaphysical, the
eternal and one. Thus, if we read the poems from a more or less

"classicist" and common-sense point of view, as evaluations of this world seen with respect to time and place, we are likely to feel some dissatisfaction, to think that some obvious things about the condition of gipsies have been overlooked or that an excessive response is being made to mere daffodils. But if we read them as symbols of man's relations to the eternal, many of these dissatisfactions disappear. This is the principal habit of reading in which Wordsworth trains us.

But there are further considerations. If the natural world is for such a poet a system of signposts telling him the way to the place he wants to go to, he is likely to feel the sort of impatience with them that we often feel with signposts: if they tell us the way to get there, they also tell us that we have not gotten there yet. They are the sign of the incompleteness of our mission. And if the objects of this world are for Wordsworth signposts to eternity, they are more than that too, they necessarily have particular and individual complexities—he must to some degree see them with relation to a fixed time and place—and this is a cause of impatience too. This impatience is likely to be reflected, for example, in the poet's use of metaphor. The goldenness of the daffodils is first of all a quality which tells us that they are charming, but it is only after the poet has abstracted himself from that golden scene that the physical gold can be converted into a much more valuable gold, "the wealth the show to [him] had brought." In one sense the wealth is the same as the gold he saw in the daffodils at first, but in another it is what that mere physical prettiness had to be *transformed into*, after a rather complex abstractive and imaginative process. If the classical poet is like a miner, sifting through the ore of his experience for its real gold, the Romantic metaphysical poet of this sort is like an alchemist, transforming petty substance into gold. He is unlike most alchemists only in that the gold he achieves may be real gold, but he is like most alchemists in that the splendor of his achievement depends on the pettiness of what he begins with. And the word "show," in the daffodils poem, illustrates this complexity too. The scene was a "show" in the sense that it was the concrete embodiment of the metaphysical joy he was looking for; but it was "only a show" in the sense that the physical scene was the appearance whose reality he was seeking and which he could find only after he had removed himself from that scene. The "inward eye" with which at last he so truly sees is in one sense the outward eye functioning at its most profound, but in another sense it is the opposite of the outward eye and depends on its closing. The "inward eye" sees at that moment when "we are laid asleep / In body, and become a living soul."

Such details illustrate very well the tension and in some respects the hostility between "surface" and "deeper" meanings in Wordsworth's poems, between symbols and what the symbols refer to, even as they illustrate the tension and in some ways the hostility between the physical and the metaphysical natures. An artist can never do entirely without the physical world, and a poet perhaps least of all. It is a condition of language that it involves willy-nilly all sorts of references and appeals not only to particular objects but to highly particularized emotions, and the complex ramifications of these are impossible for the poet utterly to resist. (Music and abstract painting, of course, have this referential quality, this tendency to concreteness, to a far lesser degree.) In later chapters we shall see some larger consequences of this problem for Wordsworth.

Our main point here is the special way in which all these considerations have led us to read the poems. It is often as if the "surface" meanings of the poems were a beautiful and intelligible message, apparent at once, and as if hidden in that message there were clues to a "deeper" meaning, still more beautiful though in some ways at odds with the message one had read at first.

Wordsworth's celebrated sonnet on Westminster Bridge is a marvelous illustration of the sort of poem which has a satisfactory meaning "with relation to a fixed time and place" and an equally wonderful, quite different meaning when understood "under the aspect of eternity":

> Earth has not anything to show more fair:
> Dull would he be of soul who could pass by
> A sight so touching in its majesty:
> This City now doth, like a garment, wear
> The beauty of the morning; silent, bare,
> Ships, towers, domes, theatres, and temples lie
> Open unto the fields, and to the sky;
> All bright and glittering in the smokeless air.

Never did sun more beautifully steep
In his first splendour, valley, rock, or hill;
Ne'er saw I, never felt, a calm so deep!
The river glideth at his own sweet will:
Dear God! the very houses seem asleep;
And all that mighty heart is lying still!

The poem is justly famous. It is a kind of dramatic monologue, in the present tense, and it seems very directly to express immediate pleasure in the eye and ear and to celebrate qualities of a particular, immediate, and personal experience, and to leave it at that, without moralizing or in any way shaking its finger at us. It is solemn without being heavy, and we are at once enchanted by the picture of London in the early morning, with its "ships, towers, domes, theatres, and temples" glittering "in the smokeless air."

The speaker is admiring London at the moment when it is least characteristic of itself, and admiring it because it is at that moment so uncharacteristic of itself. The city wears its beauty "like a garment" which covers its essential, its naked ugliness, as Duessa's ugliness was covered. There is now none of the usual smoke in the air, and the buildings lie open to the fields and sky as if they were ruins of their usual selves. A good deal of the emphasis is given not to what the city looks like but to scenes of an opposite sort, of natural country beauty, "valley, rock, and hill" at sunrise, and of a river uncluttered by the Thames' usual barges. The speaker's attitudes toward country and city, then, are the organizing notions which permit his poem to display its beautiful qualities of pathos and pleasure, the bated breath which characterizes his mood, as if his eye went on tiptoe over the scene, anxious not to awaken the city into the ugliness and confusion he hates. The speaker is a man who likes the calm and quiet of the country and dislikes the bustle of the city. His *opinions* are, in that sense, only the means by which we share his pathos and wonder at this moment, and we do not feel it necessary to agree or disagree with them. The "real subject" of the poem, by this reading, is its qualities of tone and its tactful imagery, the rendering of the particular experience, "conceived as existing with relation to a fixed time and place."

But the poem is queerer than it looks at first, and it expresses doctrines which are the antithesis, in certain ways, of the values of this particularized experience. Read in the context of his poetry as a whole, and with Wordsworth's passion for eternity in mind, the sonnet is a statement about man's essential relations to his experience and to the real, the metaphysical, nature which devaluates his temporal experience. Wordsworth's poems are major documents in the history of symbolism, which is to say that they belong to the history of an art whose "inner" or "final" or "deeper" meanings are not mere extensions or generalizations of the implications of its surface. The surface is an organization of clues to such meanings and is always to a degree depreciated by them, just as a code is in a sense depreciated by its deciphering.

This is not to say that the surface in these poems has no significance in itself. It has the significance that it has. But it is also the means to another end. The dramatic and highly particularized "surface" of the Westminster Bridge sonnet is interesting in itself, but from another point of view it is only a symbol for another set of meanings, which in themselves deny the source of values of the dramatic and the particular. Thus the last line of Wordsworth's sonnet suggests that the city is not merely sleeping but dead, its heart stilled. The poet looks at London and sees it as a sort of corpse and admires it as such, welcomes a death which is the death of what the city has come to stand for in his symbolic world. The city is a collection of men and of all their ordinary experiences, their common loves and attachments, and it therefore represents all the involvements in temporal experience from which the poet would like to escape. London awake would be the rising up of all those passions which Spinoza and Wordsworth would like to destroy or to relegate to "the smallest part of the mind." What is so beautiful to the poet about this moment early in the morning is that these passions seem for the moment to be quieted, even to be expunged. What is so full of pathos, from this point of view, is that it *is* so early in the morning, that London will inevitably awaken, that we are creatures of time, and that we have our pleasures and our pains within the limits of mortality.

The hostility between the dramatic and the symbolic readings of the poem expresses itself here in a curious observation: the "death" the poet is so pleased to witness is the death even of those properties in himself by which he responds so wonderfully to the city at this particular moment. It must always be so in the conflict between the love of eternity and the loves of time, but it is especially poignant that it should be so for a poet. It is especially moving that one of the great representatives of our human powers of articulation should be himself a lover of silence.

The reader is asked to think of such a reading as hypothetical for the reading of Wordsworth (of this period) in general, and to think of the readings which follow as the testing of that hypothesis.

CHAPTER TWO

The Love of Nature

Let me attempt a number of broad generalizations, which will be both modified and extended by what follows.

I

Man is like external nature in that both are limited by time and space: both are mortal. Man is unlike nature in that he is conscious of change, and he is also aware that at the end of the changes in his own life he must die. Thus man is conscious of himself as a separate and distinct individual in the world, who will pass away from the scene of things; and he is aware that the scene of things will survive him and will go on in its apparently endless cycles of change without him. All things that pertain to a man will pass away. All things that pertain to a flower will pass away also, but this does not seem to matter, since a flower, being—as far as man knows—unconscious of its own impending death, and even of the changes going on in itself at all times, is not a separate and distinct individual.

It must seem to man, then, that flowers and all the other non-human creatures of the world belong to another order than man: for them, change brings no individual death, since in the human sense they have no individuality, no consciousness of death. In effect, this means to man that change for them brings *no death at all.* Therefore nature can be for man a kind of metaphor for eternity, for the absence of death, and can seem to such a person as Wordsworth to possess and exemplify an order superior to his own, because it can never be the victim of the final act of personal disorder, individual death. This is the primary, or at least the simplest, source of nature's value for Wordsworth.

Consider first one of the two poems called *To a Butterfly:*

I've watched you now a full half-hour,
Self-poised upon that yellow flower;
And, little Butterfly! indeed
I know not if you sleep or feed.
How motionless!—not frozen seas
More motionless! and then
What joy awaits you, when the breeze
Hath found you out among the trees,
And calls you forth again!

This plot of orchard-ground is ours;
My trees they are, my Sister's flowers;
Here rest your wings when they are weary;
Here lodge as in a sanctuary!
Come often to us, fear no wrong;
Sit near us on the bough!
We'll talk of sunshine and of song,
And summer days, when we were young;
Sweet childish days, that were as long
As twenty days are now.

Superficially the poem is an archexample of the pathetic fallacy, deriving its charm from the tenderness the speaker lavishes on so frail a creature as he offers it a resting place safe from all harm. But in the end the speaker's assertion that the trees of this orchard are his, the flowers his sister's, seems a piece of touching effrontery, and even the assumption that he can talk to the butterfly seems a kind of impudence.

For though the poet has been watching the butterfly for half an hour, he still cannot tell if it is asleep or feeding. He cannot tell because the butterfly is more intimately involved in the rest of external nature (the yellow flower) than the man, being a man, can possibly be. The poet is excluded from the ways of butterflies, is necessarily puzzled by them and a stranger to them. For him, sleeping and feeding are separate and distinguishable activities, but for the butterfly they may not be: to sleep may be to feed, to feed to sleep. Its condition is a total peace, from which the man is excluded. This peace is the more wonderful in a creature one usually associates with constant and apparently er-

ratic motion, though it is here marvelously motionless, as motionless as "frozen seas." It is perfectly motionless, but its motionlessness is a *poise of motion*, as if the laws and impulses of change
were miraculously harmonized and brought to a stasis which is at
once motionlessness and a summation of motion, the still point of
the turning world.

Of course the speaker knows the butterfly is not forever immune to the laws of change. When the time comes, it will be found
out by the breeze and called forth from its resting place. These
terms, "found you out" and "calls you forth," suggest duty and
compulsion. But for the butterfly, to be called forth into change
is to be called forth to "joy." Its "duty" is to be joyful. For the
things of nature the laws of change and motion are in effect, just as
they are for man. But for the things of nature obedience to those
laws involves no pain.

The suggestion in the second stanza, then, that the poet's
orchard is a "sanctuary" for the butterfly is in part a delicate
irony, since it is not the butterfly that needs a sanctuary from the
breeze, from change and motion, but the man. And a closer look
reveals a deeper irony: the butterfly needs no sanctuary from
weariness or from the breeze; it needs a sanctuary from man. The
poet is promising that he and his sister will do it no harm. He is
suspending—or pretending that he *can* suspend—the ordinary
destructive element in man's relation to nature.

The speaker's asumption, in the last four lines, that he, his
sister, and the butterfly will have a kind of tea party together,
will hold a cheerful conversation, is a piece of wishful thinking,
for it assumes they all have a common relation to time and change:

> We'll talk of sunshine and of song,
> And summer days, when we were young;
> Sweet childish days, that were as long
> As twenty days are now.

The rest of the poem has so impressed us with the foreignness of
the butterfly to the man that we cannot believe what he says.
How can he converse blithely with a mystery like "frozen seas"?
The very jauntiness of the lines gives him the lie. And the last
two lines suggest that the poet's childhood bore a different rela-

tion to him than his adulthood does. Nothing in the poem suggests this was true of the butterfly. The poet's harmony with time and change ended with the end of his "sweet childish days"; for the butterfly that harmony goes on now. The poet may have been able to converse with butterflies then, but he can do so no longer.

The issue is even clearer in the other poem called *To a Butterfly*, which was composed a month earlier:

> Stay near me—do not take thy flight!
> A little longer stay in sight!
> Much converse do I find in thee,
> Historian of my infancy!
> Float near me; do not yet depart!
> Dead times revive in thee:
> Thou bring'st, gay creature as thou art!
> A solemn image to my heart,
> My father's family!
>
> Oh! pleasant, pleasant were the days,
> The time, when, in our childish plays,
> My sister Emmeline and I
> Together chased the butterfly!
> A very hunter did I rush
> Upon the prey:—with leaps and springs
> I followed on from brake to bush;
> But she, God love her! feared to brush
> The dust from off its wings.

The poem is simpler and less interesting than the other, to the degree that it makes no pretense at a community of experience between the butterfly and himself. The distinction between man and nature emerges in plain statement, not in an implicit irony. The butterfly is only a kind of memento or record of the poet's youth, and there is no pretense that even in youth the poet was any different with relation to the things of nature than he is now. Even then he was a danger to them: the butterfly was his "prey," he was a "hunter" plunging heedlessly after it. It was his sister, wiser—or younger—than himself, who took the more reverent attitude and feared "to brush / The dust from off its wings."

The butterfly here represents a principle of continuity between present and past: "Dead times revive in thee." Present and past mean nothing to a creature which, like the butterfly, possesses no individuality. (Obviously it is not even the same butterfly.) Thus, though it is "gay," it brings a "solemn image" to the heart of the poet. It reminds him of the past, when things were different, when his father was alive and days were pleasant. Present and past are different to the poet, for he is a human being, an individual, and therefore for him things come to an end. The statement that he was even then a "hunter" and a danger to butterflies is a subtle suggestion that things come to an end because he ends them. As an individual he is the enemy of butterflies, even in the innocence of his childish play; he is the enemy of continuity, and continuity—the changeless change of nonhuman nature—is his "prey."

Some lines from a poem called *Address to My Infant Daughter, Dora* [1] put this first point of ours in its most explicit form. The poem celebrates the child's first month of life, and begins with an expression of surprise that she has managed to live so long:

> —Hast thou then survived—
> Mild Offspring of infirm humanity,
> Meek Infant! among all forlornest things
> The most forlorn—one life of that bright star,
> The second glory of the Heavens?—Thou hast;
> Already hast survived that great decay,
> That transformation through the wide earth felt,
> And by all nations.

Of course she is in one sense not so forlorn: in "that Being's sight / From whom the Race of human kind proceed," her "claims extend / Through 'heaven's eternal year.'" But the poem is mainly thinking of her in terms of her physical predicament rather than in terms of her rights as God's child. Her father congratulates her on not having been born an Indian child, exposed to the elements or to a mother love less tender, more nakedly instinctual, than she is lucky enough to have, and then goes on to compare her with the moon, making a comparison which is at first favorable to the child:

> Even now—to solemnize thy helpless state,
> And to enliven in the mind's regard
> Thy passive beauty—parallels have risen,

Resemblances, or contrasts, that connect,
Within the region of a father's thoughts,
Thee and thy mate and sister of the sky.
And first;—thy sinless progress, through a world
By sorrow darkened and by care disturbed,
Apt likeness bears to hers, through gathered clouds
Moving untouched in silver purity,
And cheering oft-times their reluctant gloom.
Fair are ye both, and both are free from stain:
But thou, how leisurely thou fill'st thy horn
With brightness! leaving her to post along,
And range about, disquieted in change,
And still impatient of the shape she wears.

The moon is more obviously and immediately involved in change than the child is. But even as he says so, the father's tone darkens to a tender pity, and even a gentle irony, about the child's fate:

Once up, once down the hill, one journey, Babe,
That will suffice thee; and it seems that now
Thou hast foreknowledge that such task is thine;
Thou travellest so contentedly, and sleep'st
In such a heedless peace.

Her sleep is both unaware of the change in which she will be involved and a kind of foreknowledge of it, as if she were resting in preparation for a long and weary journey. The father's pity is given both to her innocence and to her knowledge, and it becomes explicit when he says:

Alas! full soon
Hath this conception, grateful to behold,
Changed countenance, like an object sullied o'er
By breathing mist; and thine appears to be
A mournful labour, while to her is given
Hope, and a renovation without end.

Though the moon is disquieted in change, reduced to nothing every month, she has her constant renewals, and the child has none.

These poems recognize a fundamental distinction between man and nonhuman natural things. From the point of view of man, nature can seem eternal, since its objects have no individuality and no consciousness of death; since nature's changes are cyclical, its takings away imply returns.

II

THOUGH man and nature are distinct in this way, the relations between them are not passive or indifferent, like the relations of strangers. Man's attitude toward this nature in which there appears to be no death, though he knows it undergoes changes, must necesarily be complex. He will love it, but he is himself in a unique sense a creature of time, and even its agent. He will sometimes be discovered behaving according to the laws of his own kind, as an agent of time and therefore as a destroyer of natural things.

The beautiful poem called *Nutting* [2] seems simple at first. One day, when he was a boy, Wordsworth went on a nutting expedition in the country. He came upon a peaceful grove of hazel trees, and though he enjoyed the calm and quiet of the scene for a while, eventually he went about his business of breaking the trees' branches for their produce. He was happy about having got so many of the hazelnuts but sorry that he had had to do damage to get them.

Certainly the first few lines encourage us to think of the experience as very simple:

> —It seems a day
> (I speak of one from many singled out)
> One of those heavenly days that cannot die;
> When, in the eagerness of boyish hope,
> I left our cottage-threshold, sallying forth
> With a huge wallet o'er my shoulders slung,
> A nutting-crook in hand . . .

We are led to expect only an account of some childish innocent pleasure. The child's aged teacher had dressed him in his oldest clothes and off he went, "o'er pathless rocks, / Through beds of matted fern, and tangled thickets, / Forcing my way." The verse is leisurely and relaxed, even a little garrulous:

> Tricked out in proud disguise of cast-off weeds
> Which for that service had been husbanded,
> By exhortation of my frugal Dame—
> Motley accoutrement, of power to smile
> At thorns, and brakes, and brambles,—and, in truth,
> More ragged than need was.

But as soon as the verse tells how he came upon the glade, its quality changes astonishingly. As he stood surveying the "virgin scene," he felt an anticipation like desire:

> A little while I stood,
> Breathing with such suppression of the heart
> As joy delights in; and, with wise restraint
> Voluptuous, fearless of a rival, eyed
> The banquet . . .

It is inaccurate to say only that he felt a sort of desire. Quite suddenly he *revealed himself* as having been a libertine all along, practiced and knowledgeable in the "wise restraint" that enhances pleasures, "voluptuous" and expert in it. "Eyed" sounds sinister enough, and "eyed / The banquet" suggests the habitual luxuriousness of all his tastes. He held back from taking his pleasure, not from any sense of decency or qualms of conscience or respect for the virtue of the glade, but entirely to make his later pleasure more delightful by postponing it awhile. He was able to do so because the absence of any rival, any other human being on the scene, gave him plenty of time. He was alone with his beautiful victim, the object of his desires, and she helpless before him, so he could afford to spend some time sitting beneath the trees, playing with the flowers, and allowing himself to pass into a sort of tranceful languor, in a bower

> . . . beneath whose leaves
> The violets of five seasons re-appear
> And fade, unseen by any human eye;
> Where fairy water-breaks do murmur on
> Forever . . .

The glade was enchanted ground, a fairy place, and a place where, though the changes and alterations of the seasons went on, they went on without any trouble, peacefully, the violets constantly and as it were invisibly renewing themselves under the fallen leaves, the brook murmuring on forever. It was as if he had been taken out of time. In this enchanted place he lay "in that sweet mood when pleasure loves to pay / Tribute to ease," and he was for the moment like the idle shepherd of the glade, the rocks his sheep, "fleeced with moss" and "scattered like a flock."

He fell into a kind of dream of innocence and timelessness, all for the purpose of *postponing* his ravishment of the trees:

> I heard the murmur and the murmuring sound,
> In that sweet mood when pleasure loves to pay
> Tribute to ease; and, of its joy secure,
> The heart luxuriates with indifferent things,
> Wasting its kindliness on stocks and stones,
> And on the vacant air.

But "luxuriates," and the irony in "kindliness," warn us that he is still the libertine, and when he says "*that* sweet mood," he is assuming in us a practiced libertinism like his own.

Suddenly he rose up out of his languor and "dragged to earth both branch and bough, with crash / And merciless ravage." Wantonly he destroyed the glade. (It is almost unnecessary to point out how the long, monosyllabic line shocks us at this point.) And the glade apparently accepted its destruction without a protest: the nook of hazel trees and the "green and mossy bower," though "deformed and sullied" by him, "patiently gave up / Their quiet being." His feelings about what he had done were a curious mixture: he felt a sense of pain when he "beheld the silent trees," but he was also "exulting, rich beyond the wealth of kings." The natural scene itself, which enjoys peace but can be destroyed, had a simpler response: it patiently gave up its quiet being.

The poem comes very quickly to an end, with three lines that seem quite inadequate, in tone and feeling, to the rest:

> Then, dearest Maiden, move along these shades
> In gentleness of heart; with gentle hand
> Touch—for there is a spirit in the woods.

The lines seem to have missed the point or to have got only part of it, and so to have oversimplified the rest of the poem.

A child goes out on a day's expedition in the country, with his old schoolmistress' blessing and full of the "eagerness of boyish hope," and turns out to be a sort of rapist and voluptuary in nature, the destroyer of the very peace and quiet he also enjoys. Surely the moral of this is not "Keep off the grass!" or "Don't pick the flowers!" Indeed, does the poem have a "moral" at all? Does it do any good for him to tell the maiden to treat nature gently? Isn't the poem incredible, and incredibly foolish, if we insist on regarding it as a moral injunction rather than a dispassionate analysis of man's normal and ordinary relation to his natural environment—even as a symbol or allegory of that relation? How else are we to deal with the shocking juxtaposition of the innocent and genial opening lines and the violent metaphor of lust and rapine with which his treatment of the glade is described? *All* men are like this in their relation to nonhuman nature, since *even* this innocent young child is a libertine and destroyer. The poem is able to look back on all this without making a moral judgment, and even to think of it as full of the charm of idyllic childish days, precisely because nothing can be done about it, since man and nature are there, as everywhere, demonstrating their usual and inescapable relationship. The inadequacy of the concluding lines is that they suggest a kind of judgment on the boy which is far too simple for the data. The judgment is merely arbitrary, because the boy's behavior was inevitable. It was the behavior of mankind.

Of course all this can be explained away by saying the sexual metaphor is "literary" and literally ironic, a way of emphasizing the innocence of the boy's behavior by pretending it is not innocent. But this would reduce the prevailing tone of the poem to a mere grandfatherly pastoralism about his youth, and it conflicts with what we know of Wordsworth's usual metaphorical practice. We are supposed to feel that this experience of gathering hazelnuts was *really* the experience of a voluptuary, though at the same time it was *really* only an experience of gathering hazelnuts; and that it was like all man's experience of nature, the type and symbol of a relationship between the boy as a human being and the natural scene, a relationship which could well be described by such a metaphor. It is the "virginity" of the natural scene that he loves, not merely as the boy Wordsworth but as a human being. And by his very nature as such, to love that virginity is to desire to possess it, and to possess it is to destroy it.

This is the central paradox the poem depends on. Reading it this way, we can understand why nature made it difficult for him to find the glade, why it put pathless rocks and matted fern and tangled thickets in his way—because once he found it he had necessarily to destroy it. And we can understand as well one reason why nature so "patiently gave up" its "quiet being"; nature is here acting its necessary part in a fundamental relationship. Also, there is perhaps no reason for nature to mind being "deformed and sullied," for nature has no sense, no consciousness, with which to mind it. The conflict is all in the heart of the destroyer, who in possessing the glade feels himself "rich beyond the wealth of kings." Read in this way, the line is not at all ironic, since his wealth is in the possession of all nature, his possession symbolic and total. But it *is* ironic, since in possessing nature by destroying it he possesses nothing, and since nature will reassert her ancient and peaceful order when he is gone. And he also feels a "sense of pain" upon beholding what he has done—not for any sentimental reasons but because he had valued exactly what he destroyed.

This can be understood in two ways. Man uses nature and makes his civilization out of natural things, and this use involves necessary acts of destruction. The child went out to gather hazelnuts, and by so doing practiced to be a grown-up man; nutting is a useful activity, symbolic of adulthood, and the schoolmistress' approval of the child's expedition is justified, though the expedition will make him harm the glade. The other way to understand it is far more general, and I think more characteristic of Wordsworth. Man is—not by his "civilization" and its useful acts but *by definition*—a destroyer of nonhuman nature, its definitive enemy. How he is so can best be understood by thinking of the poem as a kind of allegory of consciousness. The distinction between man and nature is a distinction between consciousness and un-consciousness of death. The human being is an agent of time. He alone, of all creatures, is self-conscious about his limitations in time, and when he brings that consciousness among things which do not have it, it is the equivalent of an act of violence against them. He is willy-nilly a destroyer or disturber of the calm of things, because he alone knows that he must die, and also that they must die. He introduces a sense of change and death where it was not before. His own feeling about this has to be complex, for it is a definition of him to say he is an agent of time, and he has to exult in his own definition; at the same time he grieves for what he has done, since peace and quietness, protection from destruction, are what he himself desires most, and therefore in ravaging the glade he has ravaged the object of his own desires.

It is not surprising that nature gives up its quiet being so patiently, since in doing so it is only playing its passive role in an essential relationship: its function is to "bend with the remover to remove." The natural scene—nonhuman nature—is perishable and unconscious of its own perishability, so it "co-operates" in its own death or change. What does the flower care if it wither up and die?

But man cares. If he is the agent of time, carrying death and change everywhere with him, he is not always a willing or loyal agent. Time oppresses him; change is his tragedy, or at least his pathos, and he is always trying to find a way of escaping into the quietness of the eternal. So he is always trying to come to terms with the eternal nature, even while he is aware of (and thus "destroying") the natural scene which is the metaphor for the eternal. He is double-natured, and he cannot avoid the implications of either side of himself. He is exiled from eternity, and his place of exile is time.

What we learn from this poem was surely hinted at in the poems we examined first: man's relation to time is not only different from that of nonhuman natural objects, he has not only a passive awareness of the fact of death which those objects apparently lack; his awareness is also active, has active consequences in his relations with the objects of the world. Wordsworth's own most striking metaphor for man's relation to nature—of marriage and of a fitting together of mind to world—begins to seem a pious hope in view of a poem like this. Man desires eternity but lives in time. Because he lives in time, and knows he does, he behaves like a creature of time and is to a degree the enemy of eternity. He can even bring his love of peace and timelessness to the service of his pleasure in time, his destructiveness. Yet his desire for a state of total rest is also perfectly genuine, and he must grieve that his very movement through time is a series of destructive acts. This helps explain why there is so little sexual imagery in Wordsworth, and why what there is tends to emphasize the destructive effects of passion. One might almost say that all human emotions except piety or awe are, in the view of these poems, destructive of nature and an obstruction to the state of eternity which, with his "best self," man desires to attain. This view, with all its complexity, is remarkably consistent throughout the major period.

I I I

IT MAY SEEM to man that the nonhuman creatures of the world belong to another order than himself: for them change apparently brings no individual death, since in the human sense they have no individuality, no consciousness of death. In effect, this means to man that change for them brings no death at all. Therefore nature can be for man a kind of symbol for eternity, for the absence of death, and can seem to such a person as Wordsworth to possess and exemplify an order superior to his own, because it can never be the victim of the final act of personal disorder, individual death.

If the mind of man could be like the natural scene, could lack the consciousness of death, would this not be, in a sense, to escape death? For a man yet alive, what is death but the consciousness of it? If nature is "conscious" not of death but of the majestic and eternal cycles of change, of passage and return, then the way for a man to learn from nature is to find in his own consciousness a corresponding region, itself unconscious of death and aware only of the cycles and interconnections of things, not of things themselves merely as things but of the relations of one thing to another, which speak to him of continuity and changelessness. And nature is not only the teacher of man, exhorting him to find such a capacity in himself, but the proving ground of that capacity. The proof of the changeless is in the seeing; nature is the place in which it can be seen.

There are several important complications here. First of all, though man has this metaphysical capacity and exercises it in his contemplations of nature, he cannot do so without interference from the other aspect of his mind, the agent of time, the awareness of death. This is his perversity, which makes him rise up in the midst of the peaceful glade and tear at the branches of the trees around him.

Second, if there is a way of looking at the natural scene by which it is a metaphor for the eternal, there are also ways of looking at it which, by emphasizing the concrete and particular, the natural objects "in themselves," demonstrate the temporality or perishability of all things. Nature may sometimes be the symbol for eternity, but it is *only* a symbol; it sometimes comes between man and the experience of eternity.

Ideally, there is in the mind of man a region which corresponds exactly to the eternal world in which he desires to dwell forever. The metaphysical experience is that moment in which the eternal world and this deepest and holiest region of man's mind merge, fuse, as it were become identified. But this is rarely possible—Wordsworth is always a little obscure about whether it is in fact possible at all. Intervening between that deepest region of man's mind and the eternal nature with which it desires identification, there are the ordinary passions and vicissitudes of the mind, those emotions and lesser reasonings which belong to and respond only to the temporal. Intervening between the objective eternal world and man is the perishable natural scene, which though it can be a symbol for eternity is nevertheless subject to change. The problem of the man who desires to be "in eternity" (before he actually dies) comes down to this: he must somehow get past or go through his own temporal passions, and past or through the temporal natural scene. He must reduce his common passions to the smallest part of the mind and look at nature as it were *sacramentally*, regarding it in the mode of eternity, responding insofar as he can only to its harmonious relations, to those things which appear least accidental and which most easily can be symbolic of eternity.

The greatness of Wordsworth's sacramentalist poems is that they never entirely deny the actuality either of the temporal passions or of the temporal natural scene. Such poems are shot through with a double consciousness of the world: they see it in the mode of time even while they struggle to see it only in the mode of eternity.

This is so generally characteristic of Wordsworth that a single example will suffice, a poem entitled *A Night-Piece:*

> —The sky is overcast
> With a continuous cloud of texture close,
> Heavy and wan, all whitened by the Moon,
> Which through that veil is indistinctly seen,
> A dull, contracted circle, yielding light
> So feebly spread that not a shadow falls,
> Checquering the ground—from rock, plant, tree, or tower.
> At length a pleasant instantaneous gleam
> Startles the pensive traveller while he treads
> His lonesome path, with unobserving eye
> Bent earthwards; he looks up—the clouds are split
> Asunder,—and above his head he sees
> The clear Moon, and the glory of the heavens.
> There, in a black-blue vault she sails along,
> Followed by multitudes of stars, that, small
> And sharp, and bright, along the dark abyss
> Drive as she drives: how fast they wheel away,
> Yet vanish not!—the wind is in the tree,
> But they are silent;—still they roll along
> Immeasurably distant; and the vault,
> Built round by those white clouds, enormous clouds,
> Still deepens its unfathomable depth.
> At length the Vision closes; and the mind,
> Not undisturbed by the delight it feels,
> Which slowly settles into peaceful calm,
> Is left to muse upon the solemn scene.

As the traveler toils along beneath the clouds, it is borne home to us how limited and dim his vision of things is. Then suddenly he is startled and amazed by a clear shaft of moonlight, and then by the dramatic sundering. He looks up at the heavens and sees the marvelous clarity of the moon and stars. Corresponding to their clarity is their silence, as if sound were the equivalent of darkness or dimness: the "wind is in the tree," but the stars "are silent." Yet he is aware of the wind in the tree at the same time that he is aware of the silence of the stars. Their distance too is emphasized: this world is the frame of dimness and cloudiness which emphasizes at once their clarity and their remoteness.

The most satisfactory way to read the poem is as a metaphor for the simultaneous operation of man's two sorts of consciousness. The clouds, the dimness of the night in which the traveler toils along, and his own earth-bent gaze, all are the ordinary conditions of his time-ridden world and his own time-ridden mind. They stand for the natural scene, which perishes around him, and express his consciousness of his own mortality, which interposes itself between him and eternity. The moon and the stars symbolize the world of eternity, the nature which does not perish, and that region of his mind which is fitted to experience such a world, the capability in him of observing and partaking of the things that endure. The word "vision" itself, with its fusion of subjective and objective, perfectly expresses the relation between the two.

For the sacramental view, ordinary nature both aids and obstructs the "vision." The clouds come between him and the moon and stars. They make his sight dim, the light of his world feeble. But when the clouds are broken, then they serve as a context by which the profundity and clarity of this vision can be emphasized. The vault the moon sails in is "built round" by them, and its depth is shown by the contrast. Just so, the silence of the stars is emphasized by the noise of the wind in the tree, which is nevertheless something of a distraction to the traveler. The moon itself, by this view, is but a symbol for the metaphysical world. It symbolizes that world adequately, by its clarity and apparent imperviousness to the vicissitudes of the earth. But it is only a symbol, it has limitations.

I V

AND NOW we come to a really formidable problem. If Wordsworth were nothing but a sacramentalist, the difficulties of his poetry would be great enough. But he was also a mystic, or rather, he believed in the validity of the mystical experience. And this made him devaluate the sacramentalist's view of things. The difference between the two views may seem small at first, as far as their effects in poetry are concerned, but it is great. It may at first seem to be a difference only in degree, but it is a difference in kind.

For the sacramentalist, nature, seen from a certain point of view, may be the *symbol* for eternity. The apparent harmony and imperviousness to individual mortality of natural things may be a sufficient guarantee of the eternal reality. For the mystic, nature can be nothing else than purely and simply an obstruction between himself and his direct contact with the eternal Presences. Nature must therefore be destroyed, obliterated absolutely. For the sacramentalist, nature is even the means to his experience of the metaphysical reality, but "experience" here, from the mystic's point of view, is only a metaphor. Really the sacramentalist is perceiving that reality from afar, so conscious is he at every moment of the context of time in which he is involved. For the mystic, the experience of eternity must mean the total abolition of his awareness of time.

We have given enough evidence, surely, of Wordsworth's sense of time to make us wary of calling him a mystic. Yet there are accounts of experiences in which the senses themselves are blotted out, the forms and images of trees and of all visible things. And Wordsworth's chief expressions for the eternal reality are ambiguous in this respect. He tends to think of it either as a sort of "harmony" or "building," or else to call it "Presences" or "Spirits." The first two terms suggest a sacramentalist view which is content to use nature as its means, since for such a view the eternal can be expressed in nature itself. The other two terms suggest a total distinction between temporal and eternal, and so are mystical, or posit the mystical experience as the only satisfactory one. Behind the appearances of things the invisible eternal waits, and its conjunctions with the mind of man are possible only in a mystery.

The distinction, as I say, may seem small at first. We noted in the previous chapter that even a sacramentalist view, even a view which is more or less satisfied with the natural scene as a symbol for the eternal, is to a degree destructive of the ordinary natural scene and the ordinary passions, since it tries to concentrate only on those aspects of things which can most readily stand for the eternal. Such a view at least *tends* toward the minimization of a complex sensuous and emotional texture in poetry. But a literally mystical view is more destructive than that: it is destructive of poetry itself, for it is destructive of all articulation. It is an experience of the unutterable, the immediate experience of *that for which there is no image.*

Now I will not argue that the evidence of Wordsworth's poetry shows he was a mystic rather than a sacramentalist. That would deny what has just been said, for the unutterable is unutterable. But, seeing the difference between the two sorts of vision, we can see that the sacramentalist was unsatisfactory to him and that the poems express over and over again a yearning for the other view, which amounts to a yearning for their own destruction. The desire for an experience of the unutterable blows like an adverse wind through the poems, and though this sometimes means the poems are the more interesting, the more moving and complex for it, it also means that the wind sometimes blows too hard, and blows the poems into contradictions of themselves or into inarticulateness.

To the Cuckoo is a marvelous case of a poem in which the two sorts of vision are brought into precarious but sucessful balance:

> O blithe New-comer! I have heard,
> I hear thee and rejoice.
> O Cuckoo! shall I call thee Bird,
> Or but a wandering Voice?
>
> While I am lying on the grass
> Thy two-fold shout I hear,
> From hill to hill it seems to pass
> At once far off, and near.
>
> Though babbling only to the Vale,
> Of sunshine and of flowers,
> Thou bringest unto me a tale
> Of visionary hours.
>
> Thrice welcome, darling of the Spring!
> Even yet thou art to me
> No bird, but an invisible thing,
> A voice, a mystery;

> The same whom in my schoolboy days
> I listened to; that Cry
> Which made me look a thousand ways
> In bush, and tree, and sky.
>
> To seek thee did I often rove
> Through woods and on the green;
> And thou wert still a hope, a love;
> Still longed for, never seen.
>
> And I can listen to thee yet;
> Can lie upon the plain
> And listen, till I do beget
> That golden time again.
>
> O blessed Bird! the earth we pace
> Again appears to be
> An unsubstantial, faery-place;
> That is fit home for Thee!

The poet's own problem in encountering the cuckoo is almost exactly our problem in reading the poem: what shall he call the bird? What is its nature as an item of his experience? "Shall I call thee Bird / Or but a wandering Voice?" The problem is never resolved in the poem, since it cannot be resolved without reducing the complexity with which the poet encounters the world. One stanza does seem to say it is only a bird in itself, but suggests it is perhaps more than a bird, other than a bird, in its effects:

> Though babbling only to the Vale,
> Of sunshine and of flowers,
> Thou bringest unto me a tale
> Of visionary hours.

Though to nature it is only a bird singing simple things, to the man, with his metaphysical capabilities, it grants the equivalent of a vision. To his sacramentalist eye the bird is a symbol of the harmony of things. But there is some pathos in this. Though it is only a simple bird to the things of nature, it comes to him as a reminder of visions he once had and has no longer, of hours he had once spent "mystically." When he says, "Even yet thou art to me / No bird," he is saying, "Of course I know better; it is a bird; it was only a childish fancy to think otherwise." But he is also saying, "Once upon a time I could think of you as you really are, as an 'invisible thing, / A voice, a mystery;' now I have fallen on evil fact-minded days, and must reduce you to a bird." He must now be satisfied with the "tale" of the "visionary hours" he once had, and he *is* satisfied, more or less. But there is bravado in *"Even yet* thou art to me / No bird," and the bird is really not quite *"the same* whom in my schoolboy days / I listened to," for really he was then naïve enough, "mystical" enough, to take the mystery literally. One of the pleasures of that "golden time," when the bird was "no bird" but a "mystery," was to search for the bird everywhere, a "thousand ways / In bush, and tree, and sky," through "woods and on the green." Of course he could not find it, because then the universe was such to him that there was no bird, the relation of human to mystery was direct and required no intermediary. This very searching was a sign that the easy "mysticism" of the golden time would come to an end; the searching took its impulse from the perverse energies of time-ridden man, by whom the universe would be filled with actual living birds, its mysteries gone forever, or available now only through the mediation of symbols.

The last line catches up most of the complexity: the effect of the bird is to transform the gross material world into an unsubstantial faery place that is "fit home" for the bird. There is an unavoidable disjunction between the world of facts and living bodies, and the world the voice sings of. Either the bird's mysterious powers are an illusion, or the world is. This is the view he has to take as an adult, since to him "mystery" has become fairy lore.

The poem depends very largely on our sense of the interplay between these two sorts of attitude, his present pleasure in what the bird signifies to him as a symbol, and his nostalgia for the time when it was no symbol but the mystery itself. We must be careful not to make our distinction too crude here. The poem does *not* express a conflict between a totally "secular" view of nature and a "metaphysical" one. The poet has not lost his ability to value the mystery. The poem expresses a conflict between two sorts of metaphysical attitudes, the "sacramental" and the "mys-

tical," the one present, the other past. The poem does not say that
the bird is no longer an adequate symbol for the eternal reality,
the mystery. There is never any doubt about what the bird stands
for, or that it stands for it adequately. The poem rather yearns
for the time when the bird was not a symbol at all, but the mystery
itself, literally. It yearns for the time when the world expressed
more truth than poetry is capable of.

v

LET US recast this more particularly in stylistic terms. The image
of the bird is, in an exact Coleridgean sense, *symbolic*. But its
value as such is at least in part rejected.

Coleridge says that a symbol is a "translucent" instance, which,
"while it enunciates the whole, abides itself as a living part of
that unity of which it is the representative." [3] Again, speaking of
nature, he says:

> But it has been the music of gentle and pious minds in all ages, it
> is the poetry of all human nature, to read it likewise in a figurative
> sense, and to find therein correspondences and symbols of the spir-
> itual world. [4]

Looking at a particular scene, he says:

> I seem to myself to behold in the quiet objects, on which I am
> gazing, more than an arbitrary illustration, more than a mere
> *simile*, the work of my own fancy. I feel an awe, as if there were
> before my eyes the same power as that of the reason—the same
> power in a lower dignity, and therefore a symbol established in the
> truth of things. [5]

And again:

> That which we find in ourselves is . . . the substance and life of
> all our knowledge. Without this latest presence of the "I am," all
> modes of existence in the external world would flit before us as
> colored shadows, with no greater depth, root, or fixture, than the
> image of a rock hath in a gliding stream or the rainbow on a fast-
> sailing rainstorm. The human mind is the compass, in which the
> laws and actuations of all outward essences are revealed as the dips

and declinations. . . . True natural philosophy is comprized in the study of the science and language of symbols. The power delegated to nature is all in every part: and by a symbol I mean, not a metaphor or allegory or any other figure of speech or form of fancy, but an actual and essential part of that, the whole of which it represents.[6]

This theory of symbolism posits as its ground the double consciousness we have been speaking of, whereby the objects of nature may have individual and particular identity in themselves as objects, yet will stand "figuratively" for the whole of which they really are part. The world of perishable things is, to be sure, a "gliding stream" or a "fast-sailing rainstorm," unless we see its rocks and lights symbolically, as referents to and substantive with the eternal world. But the world of perishable things is praised because it can be so regarded.

There is no operation of the will discernible in the symbolic figure, for its guarantee is neither the tactical nor strategic literary motives of its author but its truth in nature. The symbolic poet uses his symbol because he is *compelled by its truth* to use it. Nor does this mean that a symbol is "objective" and a metaphor "subjective," for it is the very nature of symbols to destroy such a distinction: "That which we find in ourselves . . . is the substance and life of our knowledge"; the mind discovers in itself the truth of what it sees outside itself. We gain an insight here, for example, into the phrase "inward eye," in *I wandered lonely as a cloud.* The poet records the data of his experience with his outward eye, but his "inward eye" sees deeper into the truth of things. In what direction does it look? In two at once: deeper into the landscape, as it were, behind or through the mere physical presence of the daffodils; and deeper into that region of the mind where all things are eternal, where the very structure and laws of nature can be discerned.

The symbol is what art is, for art is symbol. And art is the "mediatress between, and reconciler of, nature and man." And nature, for these purposes, is "the beautiful in nature"; and the beautiful in nature is, "in the abstract, the unity of the manifold, the coalescence of the diverse; in the concrete, it is the union of the shapely . . . with the vital." [7]

So far, Coleridge and Wordsworth are undoubtedly alike. But there is a difference, which can be got at by going back to Coleridge's observation that a symbol is always a "part" of what it represents. This suggests not only that tenor and vehicle in a symbolic figure are related with an intimacy unavailable to a metaphor. It also suggests—what may at first seem surprising— that a symbol is always of *less* magnitude than what it represents. Small wonder, since in both Wordsworth and Coleridge the symbol "represents" the whole perfection of things, the eternal reality itself. But here there is the difference between the two men.

There is an interesting passage in Coleridge, which may or may not represent a consistent view in his work but which is illuminating here. He says:

> For we know that the whole creation groaneth and travaileth in earnest expectation (Rom. VIII. 20–23) of a renewal of its forfeited power, the power, namely, of retiring into that image, which is its substantial form and true life, from the variety of self, which then only is when for itself it hath ceased to be.[8]

What the whole creation groans for and expects is to be transformed into that final summary of itself which is at once its self and its most perfect image, the eternal world which is without change and without contradictions, when the symbol will no longer be of less magnitude than what it represents—when, in fact, there will be no symbol at all, since creation will have retired into its own perfection. Then there will be no art, since there will be no need of a mediatress between nature and man.

What this implies may be implicit also in his remark:

> There is a difference between form as proceeding, and shape as superinduced;—the latter is either the death or the imprisonment of the thing;—the former is its self-witnessing and self-affected sphere of agency. Art would or should be the abridgement of nature. Now the fulness of nature is without character, as water is the purest when without taste, smell, or color; but this is the highest, the apex only,—it is not the whole.[9]

Which is to say, it is not the whole story. The fullness of nature is not yet. Coleridge sees the possibility, at the end of historical time, of a paradisal state in which there will be no conflict between heaven and earth or between men and things, in which reality will be as the purest water, tasteless, colorless, odorless— in which, that is to say, there will be no necessity of the intermediaries of sense and feeling between men and reality. The function of art, by this view, is to discover and reiterate this great promise in nature, and the symbols of art express the summation and ideal image toward which history is moving, while at the same time they express the fact that it has not got there *yet*.

We can perhaps be clearer by oversimplifying intellectual history and saying that this aspect of Coleridge's theory distinguishes him from a mechanistic or—in the popular sense—"Newtonian" view. Such a view is symbolic too, in its way, since it sees the world not only in its particulars but as its order, and by regarding any instance of order or relationship it can perceive a symbol of the order of all things, of God's handiwork. But it sees that order as static, as an order always present in time and not fully recognizable by man only because of the frailty or limitation of his vision:

> Cease then, nor Order Imperfection name:
> Our proper bliss depends on what we blame.
> Know thy own point: This kind, this due degree
> Of blindness, weakness, Heav'n bestows on thee.[10]

Coleridge sees "form as proceeding," order as a process of development toward regaining nature's "forfeited power" of "retiring into that image, which is its substantial form and true life." His vision of order is thus both present in time and future in time, the union of "the shapely . . . with the vital."

But if this vision distinguishes Coleridge from the mechanists, it distinguishes him also from Wordsworth. Coleridge is talking in the way I have described as sacramentalist. The things of nature are divine in that they abide in and are part of what they represent. But they are *not* divine in that they are now only *part* of what they represent, not yet retired into it. His theory of symbolism thus depends upon a consistent sense of the present corruption or incompleteness of this world and of man's life in this world, and it leaves no room for kicking against the pricks, no room for the adverse wind of a mystical yearning.

Wordsworth subscribes to this view except in one important respect: there may be times in a man's life, there almost certainly *have been* times, when he is able to make direct contact with the metaphysical reality without mediation on the part of nature. Coleridge's view of things promises "experience," or at least knowledge, of the eternal, for he promises that nature is symbolic —which is to say that it really abides in the truth of things as part of that truth. This knowledge is possible by means of the sacramental reason, or imagination, which can train itself by piety and discipline to look at nature as nearly as possible in her symbolic aspects. But how disappointing, how less-than-enough, this must be for one who has known the infinite immediately, and for whom nature has therefore at one time or another not existed! Coleridge promises an end to symbolism at the end of historical time; Wordsworth says it has ended, and perhaps can end, in biographical time, in personal experience; or at least—one hardly knows how to say it—he so wishes that this were true that he distrusts and disvalues the very symbols he perceives. He is a sacramentalist like Coleridge, but unwillingly, grudgingly, and he sometimes turns on his own symbolism and devours it.

How often the mystical experience of things was made actual for Wordsworth—or whether it was ever made actual at all—is very difficult to say. The poetry gives remarkably little evidence of it, even ambiguously, and it shows itself there principally as what I have called the "mystical yearning," an element in the verse itself which seems dissatisfied with the sacramentalist view of things, as Wordsworth was dissatisfied with the present function of the cuckoo and hearkened back to the time when it was no bird at all to him—when, that is, the symbol had no temporal part, no "vehicle," at all.

All this may, for example, help explain Coleridge's famous puzzlement over the child-philosopher in the great Ode.[11] He asks in what sense it can be a "philosopher," or *read* "'the eternal deep,'" or deserve the splendid titles of "a *mighty prophet*, a *blessed seer*." He wonders at what time "were we dipped in the Lethe, which has produced such utter oblivion of a state so godlike?" And he says:

In what sense can the magnificent attributes, above quoted, be appropriated to a *child*, which would not make them equally suitable to a *bee*, or a *dog*, or a *field of corn*: or even to a ship, or to the wind and waves that propel it? The omnipresent Spirit works equally in them, as in the child; and the child is equally unconscious of it as they.[12]

I. A. Richards defends Wordsworth by asking why he should "deny that, in a much less degree, these attributes are equally suitable to a bee, or a dog, or a field of corn." He quotes Coleridge's "amends" for his cavils:

> The ode was intended for such readers only as had been accustomed to watch the flux and reflux of their utmost nature, to venture at times into the twilight realms of consciousness, and to feel a deep interest in modes of inmost being, to which they know that the attributes of time and space are inapplicable and alien, but which yet cannot be conveyed save in symbols of time and space. For such readers the sense is sufficiently plain, and they will be as little disposed to charge Mr Wordsworth with believing the Platonic pre-existence in the ordinary interpretation of the words, as I am to believe, that Plato himself ever meant or taught it.[13]

But this is treating the poem as if it were what Coleridge might have wanted it to be, a thoroughgoing sacramentalist document containing no element of mystical yearning. Wordsworth says what he says about the child not because it is just another convenient image drawn from within the limits of time and space, to body forth things which could not be expressed any other way. He says it because a child, which is a human being, has a different and more complicated relation to eternity than other kinds of created beings.

A bee, a dog, or a wave, as temporal objects spatially limited, can express symbolically the truth of things, which is always the perfect union of temporal and eternal. They are, furthermore, in their lack of knowledge of their own mortality, even the *equivalents* of mystics. But only a human being is committed to a painful separation from the eternal truth of things, and only the human being can imagine a state of mind in which he was identified with the truth of things. So that it is meaningful to talk about a perfect union with eternity only in terms of the human mystical experience. For nonhuman natural objects the problem simply does not arise. A bee, a dog, or a wave can be images of a mystical relation to things, and when a human being is most successfully "mystical" he is most successfully like the other objects of nature. But the problem is always double: Wordsworth is always talking at once about man's mystical possibilities and about his failure to fulfill them, and for this purpose only the child, the human being, can be the hero of his poem. Only in the figure of the child can Wordsworth bring together his ambivalent or ambiguous attitudes about mortality, his sense of the perfection that was lost, and his contradictory sense of the values that have been gained by losing it. This is suggested best by the troubled tone of his own comments on the poem (dictated in 1843 to Miss Fenwick), in which he defends his use of the doctrine of "pre-existence":

> Nothing was more difficult for me in childhood than to admit the notion of death as a state applicable to my own being. I have said elsewhere—
>
> > 'A simple child,
> > That lightly draws its breath,
> > And feels its life in every limb,
> > What should it know of death!'—
>
> But it was not so much from [feelings] of animal vivacity that *my* difficulty came as from a sense of the indomitableness of the spirit within me. I used to brood over the stories of Enoch and Elijah, and almost to persuade myself that, whatever might become of others, I should be translated, in something of the same way, to heaven. With a feeling congenial to this, I was often unable to think of external things as having external existence, and I communed with all that I saw as something not apart from, but inherent in, my own immaterial nature. At that time I was afraid of such processes. In later periods of life I have deplored, as we have all reason to do, a subjugation of an opposite character, and have rejoiced over the remembrances, as is expressed in the lines—
>
> > 'Obstinate questionings
> > Of sense and outward things,
> > Fallings from us, vanishings;' etc.

To that dream-like vividness and splendour which invest objects of sight in childhood, every one, I believe, if he would look back, could bear testimony, and I need not dwell upon it here: but having in the Poem regarded it as presumptive evidence of a prior state of existence, I think it right to protest against a conclusion, which has given pain to some good and pious persons, that I meant to inculcate such a belief. It is far too shadowy a notion to be recommended to faith as more than an element in our instincts of immortality. But let us bear in mind that, though the idea is not advanced in revelation, there is nothing there to contradict it, and the fall of Man presents an analogy in its favor.[14]

It was an "abyss of idealism," yet it is important to deplore a "subjugation of an opposite character," which would entirely deny it. It is "far too shadowy a notion to be recommended to faith," but this is qualified by the end of the sentence; and besides, "far too shadowy" does not say it is untrue, it only says it is not very useful for supporting faith in others. There are no grounds for it in Scripture, but there is nothing there to contradict it either. And "abyss" is a word he uses many times to suggest the hiding place of ultimate truths, and rarely uses elsewhere, so far as I know, in a pejorative sense.

Certainly the passage cannot be read as a simple statement that he used the belief only as a convenience, to express something else. Coleridge's uneasiness with the image of the child has some grounds, then. He felt in it the distinction between his own sacramentalist view of things and Wordsworth's mystical yearning. The bee, the dog, the wave, are not equally suitable with the child, in that all can be symbolic of the "omni-present Spirit." The child brings more into the poem than that. It is a human being in a special state of grace, as yet unfallen or only just beginning its fall, and it bears a mystical relation to the eternal which could not be shared by the bee, the dog, or the wave, for its perfection is meaningful in view of the fact that it will be lost, that human experience involves a sort of pain which other creatures never experience. They can symbolize the relation of time to eternity, but the child is never precisely a symbol, never simply the visible manifestation of what it represents, as part of what it represents.

The structure of the Ode is characterized by two opposite movements, which pass through and contradict one another. One of these, the movement of growth through time to individual death, we can call by our term "sacramentalist." The other, the movement backward through childhood to eternity, we can call by our term "mystical yearning."

Lionel Trilling in his excellent essay on the Ode distinguishes very clearly between the two movements, though in ways significantly different from my own. His essay serves as a useful guide into the intricacies of the poem. He is concerned to combat the view that the poem is "Wordsworth's farewell to his art," and he argues that, quite to the contrary, "it is a welcome of new power and a dedication to a new poetic subject." [15] The poem is about growing up, and about the exchange of one sort of power for another—and perhaps more important, about the exchange of one attitude toward life for another. Mr. Trilling defines these attitudes in what he calls "naturalistic" terms:

> I have tried to be as naturalistic as possible in speaking of Wordsworth's childhood experiences and the more-or-less Platonic notion they suggested to him. I believe that naturalism is in order here, for what we must now see is that Wordsworth is talking about something common to us all, the development of the sense of reality. To have once had the visionary gleam of the perfect union of the self and the universe is essential to and definitive of our human nature, and it is in that sense connected with the making of poetry. But the visionary gleam is not in itself the poetry-making power, and its diminution is right and inevitable. [16]

The "visionary gleam" is being exchanged, then, for the "sense of reality." The "visionary gleam" refers to the time in one's life when one feels a perfect union with the universe, so that the world outside one's self appears not in itself to be actual at all. The "sense of reality" is in effect the result of what one learns as one grows up—that there is a distinction between one's self and the universe, and that the distinction must, in the interests of maturity, be accepted. In a moment I will quarrel with Mr. Trilling's naturalistic terms, but they define, so far as they go, what I take to be the antipodes of the range of experience described by the poem.

Mr. Trilling is quite aware that the poem takes a complex view of this exchange of power for power:

simultaneous conflict

That there should be ambivalence in Wordsworth's response to this diminution is quite natural, and the two answers, that of stanzas V–VIII and that of stanzas IX–XI, comprise both resistance to and acceptance of growth. Inevitably we resist change and turn back with passionate nostalgia to the stage we are leaving. Still, we fulfill ourselves by choosing what is painful and difficult and necessary, and we develop by moving toward death. In short, organic development is a hard paradox which Wordsworth is stating in the discrepant answers of the second part of the Ode. And it seems to me that those critics who made the Ode refer to some particular and unique experience of Wordsworth's and who make it relate only to poetical powers have forgotten their own lives and in consequence conceive the Ode to be a lesser thing than it really is, for it is not about poetry, it is about life. And having made this error, they are inevitably led to misinterpret the meaning of the "philosophic mind" and also to deny that Wordsworth's ambivalence is sincere. No doubt it would not be a sincere ambivalence if Wordsworth were really saying farewell to poetry, it would merely be an attempt at self-consolation. But he is not saying farewell to poetry, he is saying farewell to Eden, and his ambivalence is much what Adam's was, and Milton's, and for the same reasons.[17]

Mr. Trilling is quite right when he says that those who call the poem Wordsworth's farewell to his art conceive it to be a lesser thing than it is, and I think he is right when he says the ambivalence in it would not be sincere if that were all it meant. But I also think his argument loses something by its "naturalism" and by not distinguishing between one sort of imagination—the "poetry-making power"—and another. I agree that the Ode is about life but insist that it is also about poetry. It is a poem about life by a man for whom, in the most radical sense, life was imagination, and one result of imagination was poetry.

Imagination, for both Wordsworth and Coleridge, has to be defined first of all not in terms of what gets into literary works of art, nor in terms of how they are shaped, but in terms of the relation of man to nature. We saw earlier that Coleridge's theory of symbolism and his theory of art depend on his rigorous acceptance of the actuality of temporal nature, since temporal nature is symbolic of eternal nature and *could not be so if it were not temporal*—a symbol abides in the truth of things and enunciates the whole of which it is part. It could not do so if it were identified with the whole. Wordsworth's theory of *art* certainly does not differ from this. Mr. Trilling is right when he says that, far from being a lament over the loss of poetic power, the Ode is a welcome of new powers. He is right, in another paragraph, to find the source of these powers in a new awareness of "man's mortality" which makes the world "significant and precious." [18] But I think he is wrong to leave it at that. The welcome to new powers in the poem is a welcome to the symbol-making, or rather the symbol-*accepting*, powers of the imagination, for it is an acceptance of the actuality of our ordinary natural environment, and therefore of its temporality, and therefore of the conditions under which symbolism is possible and necessary:

> Earth fills her lap with pleasures of her own;
> Yearnings she hath in her own natural kind,
> And, even with something of a Mother's mind,
>   And no unworthy aim,
>   The homely Nurse doth all she can
> To make her Foster-child, her Inmate Man,
>   Forget the glories he hath known,
> And that imperial palace whence he came.

When Wordsworth says, in the last stanza of the poem, that he is willing to "live beneath" the "more habitual sway" of the "Fountains, Meadows, Hills, and Groves," and of the brooks and natural sunrise, he is making a moral statement, for he is accepting man's limitations in time and space, but he is making a statement about the conditions of poetry too. When he says, "To me the meanest flower that blows can give / Thoughts that do often lie too deep for tears," we are certainly meant to take the statement as moral, as referring back to "soothing thoughts that spring / Out of human suffering"; but we ought to read it finally, I think, as a statement of the acceptance of temporal nature as the repository of symbols—as the only way left, for a man who has lost his mystical capabilities, to have an experience of the eternal.

If we take as our essential and simplest definition of imagination the power which *somehow or other* makes contact with the eternal reality, then the "visionary gleam" possessed by infants— the direct and immediate and easy relation to the eternal which is lost as soon as "shades of the prison-house begin to close"— then this visionary gleam is imagination too, but of a higher sort, and the poem is indeed, though not a farewell to his art, a dirge sung over his departing imaginative powers. The poem is, in fact, really a lament over the *gain* of poetic power, or rather of that sort of imagination, for it is a formal and reluctant acceptance of the limiting conditions under which poetry is possible. If mortal man can relate himself to the eternal only through the mediation of symbols, and mortal nature is the repository of symbols, then poetry—vision by means of symbols—is the only imaginative means available to him. But if the poet really believes that there was a time when his relation to the eternal did not need the mediation of symbols, then he must always be impelled to lament that time as having possessed and made use of a higher form of imagination than poetry.

Nature is at once the source of power for such a poet, since it is the source of his symbols, and a limitation, since his awareness of it is his acknowledgment that he is mortal. There is a wonderful irony, then, in the second stanza, in its emphasis on the *present* beauty of the world to the poet:

> The Rainbow comes and goes,
> And lovely is the Rose,
> The Moon doth with delight
> Look round her when the heavens are bare;
> Waters on a starry night
> Are beautiful and fair;
> The sunshine is a glorious birth;
> But yet I know, where'er I go,
> That there hath past away a glory from the earth.

Nothing could seem more wholehearted than this praise of the natural world. But the last line does not say that the world of nature has, as such, become less beautiful to him than it ever was; it says, in the context of the whole poem, that its very beauty, its very presence, is the sign to him that a "glory" he had known

once has passed away. The glory he had known is the very antithesis of these pleasures of the mortal vision:

> Not for these I raise
> The song of thanks and praise;
> But for those obstinate questionings
> Of sense and outward things,
> Fallings from us, vanishings. . . .

The infant's sight is of a different order than the man's; it turns
the world of ordinary sight into a "dream" and thus in a way
obliterates it. The limitation of the symbolic imagination, which
must work through nature and must be aware of nature's temporality, is that it cannot see things as if they were not there—
it cannot make them vanish. Its seeing is all through mediations;
the poet can hear the trumpets of glory, to be sure, but only in
the cataracts, or echoed and having to pierce mountains to reach
him. Though his sacramental vision can even make him feel that
he has been brought near to the immortal sea "from which we
came," when he gets there, visiting it more or less as a stranger,
he discovers there the children, those mystics, sporting on the
shore, quite at home and able to be irresponsible, because they are,
for the time, at one with it.

The poet's imagination is limited in space, because mountains
and cataracts, roses and rainbows, and even the moon, get between
him and fullest knowledge of the eternal. It is limited in time because even his sacramental knowledge is but fitful and keeps
falling away. Children and lambs, because they are unconscious of
mortality, can sport in nature in perfect harmony with it, and with
both kinds of nature, temporal and eternal, for they see no disjunction between the two. The poet can for a time feel that he is
sharing their innocent wisdom, but even then he has to say:

> —But there's a Tree, of many, one,
> A single Field which I have looked upon,
> Both of them speak of something that is gone:
> The Pansy at my feet
> Doth the same Tale repeat:
> Whither is fled the visionary gleam?
> Where is it now, the glory and the dream?

The yearning for the mystical childhood relation to nature destroys the grown-up sacramental or symbolic vision, since it is always finding it unsatisfactory, the exercise of a lower power than the poet once possessed.

Mr. Trilling says it is quite natural that there should be ambivalence in the poem, and certainly it is—the poem makes us feel that its ambivalence is the inevitable product of its main issues. But Mr. Trilling seems to indicate that the decision finally goes to the acceptance of mortality, of what I call the "sacramental imagination," and about this I think one cannot be so sure. Is there not a kind of vagueness in "thoughts that do often lie too deep for tears," and in "the soothing thoughts that spring / Out of human suffering," and indeed a kind of sublime sour grapes about the conclusion in general; and is this vagueness and suspicious optimism contemplated or contained quite successfully by the poem as a whole?

I think the vagueness derives at once from the prevailing elegiac tone of the poem and from its failure really to convince us that the childhood vision of things *is* the "fountain-light of all our day," the "master light of all our seeing." Hasn't the poem labored to persuade us that the "light" by which children see and in which they are bathed, the light they share with the unconscious lamb and the flowers, is different in *kind* from the light of common day? Is our adult light really but a diminution of the same light by which the infant philosopher sees the truth? Is it not rather a different and inferior *sort* of light, which really is as darkness to the light of infancy, as blindness to the infant vision? This is not to say that we do not see the truth with our adult vision, though only fitfully and occasionally. It is to say that we see it by an utterly different means, and that the poem's attempt to assert otherwise remains but an assertion, though a marvelously powerful and moving one. The key metaphors really do contradict one another, and we have to choose between them: if there is something "in our embers" "that doth live," then we are not really as the blind compared to the child, nor as the dead to the child's life. A dying fire is one thing, blindness and death are others.

And the poem is vague also about another matter—the way the adult compromise, the sacramental or symbolic vision, becomes moral, the way it leads to what Mr. Trilling calls a "new poetic subject-matter," the "thoughts that do often lie too deep for tears." I think nearly everyone will read that line, and the lines about the philosophic mind and the thoughts that spring out of suffering, as indicating that one effect of adulthood is to lead one to turn one's attention to one's fellow man, to say farewell, as Mr. Trilling remarks, to the "egotistical sublime." But here we have to ask the same question: how does the childhood mysticism, the power one has to give up, lead to the adult love of man? And the same question, in another more crucial form: how does the "sacramental vision," this new way of experiencing the eternal through the agency of temporal nature, lead to the love of man? The poem really only asserts that this is so. It makes a claim without being able to describe the process by which the claim is justified.

V I

ALL THIS brings us back to the question which introduced this chapter: how does the "love of nature" lead to the "love of man"? We can now, with a sufficient sense of the complexities involved, define the "love of nature" either as the "mystical" relation of the child or the "sacramental" relation of the adult to the eternal. And we can now, with some confidence, describe both relations as aspects of the imagination. But how is the love of nature, in either of these senses, able to lead to the love of man? And what definition of man is intended, would have to be intended, in such a statement? These are the questions which guide our discussion in the next chapter. And the point of the next chapter—the main point, anyway—is that the first question cannot be answered unless we are willing to accept a definition of man by which he is enlarged— or reduced—to a glorious abstraction and simplification of himself, the exponent purely of his metaphysical capability.

CHAPTER THREE

The Love of Man

THE TWO POINTS of view, sacramentalist and mystical, are alike both in their insistence that there is an eternal nature, and in their corresponding insistence that there is in man a psychological capacity to apprehend the eternal. It follows, from our account of the divergence between the two views of nature, that there will be a corresponding divergence between their attitudes toward, their definitions of, this psychological capacity in man. This chapter, then, which is concerned with the "love of man" and with defining the process by which, as Wordsworth says, the love of nature leads to the love of man, will tell us nothing really new. But the poems are there, and it is necessary to talk about them, since they are so beautiful and interesting. And, though the problems raised here, when stated abstractly, are nothing new, they have a peculiar relevance and significance in poems dealing with human beings. Wordsworth's readers are human beings, and the grand question is always the question of a poet's relevance to human lives. Wordsworth is in a certain sense the most remote of our great poets from the ordinary reader. If this book has anything important to say about him, it will come from the labor of documenting such a remark. Here is a poet whose works are full of images of human beings, and full too of insistences that he is dealing with the elemental, the essential and abiding passions of the human heart. He has been praised as the poet of the primary affections and of simple feelings. My argument about him comes down to this, that he is far from being such a poet. He is not the poet of the human heart, nor of the relations between human beings—unless we are willing to accept his own extraordinary definitions of those things. And when Arnold says of him, "He spoke, and loos'd our hearts in tears," he is talking about some other poet, easy to mistake for

Wordsworth and traveling under his name, but another poet nevertheless. Wordsworth's yearning for an uncorrupted experience of the eternal is so intense and powerful that it ends in the devaluation of our ordinary experience, even in the desire for its destruction. In this sense, and if we stubbornly define humanity not merely by the metaphysical capacity Wordsworth ascribes to men but also by their intricate and moving involvements in the accidents of space and time, Wordsworth is not a great lover of man but almost a great despiser of him.

It cannot be denied that the subject matter, or the apparent subject matter, of most of the poems is the sorrows and joys of human beings in "ordinary" circumstances. It cannot be denied that Wordsworth's poems often have all the appearance of being celebrations of the pleasures and pains of the human heart. But it will be possible to demonstrate how this apparent subject matter is a kind of cipher or hieroglyph for meanings which reject or devaluate the very experiences which express them. The tenors of his metaphors tend to reject their vehicles. The symbolic meanings of his poems tend to reject their sensuous, dramatic surfaces.

To return to the problem at hand: the two dominant views of nature in Wordsworth are both metaphysical, yet the one thwarts and denies the other—the mystical thwarts the sacramental—for the one depends as much on the obliteration of our temporal and spatial limitations as the other depends on their existence. Both views presuppose a capacity in man to apprehend, one way or another, the metaphysical reality. But the two views, being so different from one another, must necessarily regard this metaphysical capacity in radically different ways. And they do so in the same poems. The two attitudes arise from the same source, their common belief in an eternal metaphysical reality. And they both agree that the easy mystical childhood relation to this reality is lost as one grows older. But here they diverge, for while the sacramentalist view promises that something of that relation can be retained by the development within us of our symbolic powers, our powers of reading the symbols of our natural environment, the other view is not satisfied with this and rages for the lost mysticism. For the sacramentalist view, then, man's metaphysical capacity is his symbol-making or symbol-reading power, the power best exemplified by the poetic imagination. For the other view,

this psychological capacity is the very opposite of the poetic imagination, which depends on temporal nature as its reservoir of symbols: the mystical imagination is a hater of temporal nature.

I

IN A WAY, all this is the end of our argument, not the beginning,
and we have put the cart before the horse. The "man" the love of
nature leads us to love is one of two antithetical heroes, the hero
of the sacramentalist imagination, who is the poet, and the hero
of the mystical imagination, who is the child, the old man, the idiot,
the simple inarticulate peasant. In many of the poems these
heroes are confused and merged into one. Before we can substan-
tiate such remarks, it is necessary first to look at some evidence
of what seems to be a fairly simple antipathy to other men on
Wordsworth's part, and a hostility to man's commitment to the
ordinary functions of life.

Let us begin, moreover, by looking at a series of poems, the
sonnet series called *Personal Talk*, where his antipathy seems not
to come from his doctrine of nature but the other way around, as
if it were visceral and the product of an emotional bent, a hostile
disposition in the blood. The most extraordinary of the four poems
in this respect is the first:

> I am not One who oft or much delight
> To season my fireside with personal talk,—
> Of friends, who live within an easy walk,
> Or neighbours, daily, weekly, in my sight:
> And, for my chance-acquaintance, ladies bright,
> Sons, mothers, maidens withering on the stalk,
> These all wear out of me, like Forms, with chalk
> Painted on rich men's floors, for one feast-night.
> Better than such discourse doth silence long,
> Long barren silence, square with my desire;
> To sit without emotion, hope, or aim,
> In the loved presence of my cottage-fire,
> And listen to the flapping of the flame,
> Or kettle whispering its faint undersong.

Wordsworth rather spitefully said he had a spite against this poem
because it nearly lost him the friendship of "dear Miss Fenwick,

who has always stigmatised one line of it as vulgar, and worthy
only of having been composed by a country Squire." [1] But if she
took "maidens withering on the stalk" too much to heart, if the
shoe fitted and she put it on, we can surely feel more sympathy
with her than Wordsworth apparently did. Her criticism is just,
and it has applications beyond the particular line. Friends and
acquaintances are to him "like Forms, with chalk / Painted on
rich men's floors, for one feast-night": they are at best an indulgence, and perhaps a suspect indulgence at that, like the luxuriousness of the rich; they are substanceless things, chalk outlines of
human beings; and the personal discourse with them is itself what
wears them out, just as the dancers in the rich man's house wear
out the chalk drawings on the floor by their dancing. Wordsworth
is going to say later on that he prefers to them the company of the
"nobler loves, and nobler cares" given us by poets. But he makes
an astonishing confession when he says here that he prefers *barren*
silence and to sit alone "without emotion, hope, or aim," in a kind
of vacancy of thought and feeling, before his cottage fire. There
is a gratuitous and pathetic ill temper about this which seems anything but intentional, anything but part of the dramatic design.

The second sonnet makes it plainer how the cards are stacked:

> "Yet life," you say, "is life; we have seen and see,
> And with a living pleasure we describe;
> And fits of sprightly malice do but bribe
> The languid mind into activity.
> Sound sense, and love itself, and mirth and glee
> Are fostered by the comment and the gibe."
> Even be it so: yet still among your tribe,
> Our daily world's true Worldlings, rank not me!
> Children are blest, and powerful; their world lies
> More justly balanced; partly at their feet,
> And part far from them:—sweetest melodies
> Are those that are by distance made more sweet;
> Whose mind is but the mind of his own eyes,
> He is a Slave; the meanest we can meet!

We may be inclined to draw in our criticism a little when it seems
by the first lines that he is only talking about *malicious* conversation, the "comment and the gibe." But what he holds up against

this sort of talk is not another and better sort, but the fancies of children, living part in this world and part in the world of make-believe. The "tribe" he scorns includes all adults, and his scorn for the "you" who represents that tribe seems fantastically excessive. The world the speaker recommends is one as far as possible from the world of present situations and social intercourse, and to that world we fly on wings of the imagination, which finds its satisfactions either in the contemplation of nature or in books:

> Wings have we,—and as far as we can go
> We may find pleasure: wilderness and wood,
> Blank ocean and mere sky, support that mood
> Which with the lofty sanctifies the low.
> Dreams, books, are each a world; and books, we know,
> Are a substantial world, both pure and good:
> Round these, with tendrils strong as flesh and blood,
> Our pastime and our happiness will grow.
> There find I personal themes, a plenteous store,
> Matter wherein right voluble I am,
> To which I listen with a ready ear;
> Two shall be named, pre-eminently dear,—
> The gentle Lady married to the Moor;
> And heavenly Una with her milk-white Lamb.

The world of books is "substantial," we are to understand, by contrast to the world of social intercourse, which is a world of chalk forms; and the world of books is substantial—so the syntax of the line suggests—because it is "pure and good," because it is an ideal world whose purest and best, thus most substantial, figures are Una and Desdemona, both passive and innocent victims of their respective worlds. Our "pastime and our happiness" will grow around the world of books with "tendrils strong as flesh and blood," and infinitely more to be admired because they are *not* flesh and blood.

The final sonnet rises to an apostrophe of the poets, which however has some disturbing implications:

> Nor can I not believe but that hereby
> Great gains are mine; for thus I live remote
> From evil-speaking; rancour, never sought,
> Comes to me not; malignant truth, or lie.

> Hence have I genial seasons, hence have I
> Smooth passions, smooth discourse, and joyous thought:
> And thus from day to day my little boat
> Rocks in its harbour, lodging peaceably.
> Blessings be with them—and eternal praise,
> Who gave us nobler loves, and nobler cares—
> The Poets, who on earth have made us heirs
> Of truth and pure delight by heavenly lays!
> Oh! might my name be numbered among theirs,
> Then gladly would I end my mortal days.

He lives remote from evil-speaking because he lives as remote as possible from any speaking at all; he feels no rancor toward anything and is the object of none, because he stays out of the arena where rancor is possible. And his rewards are *"smooth* passions" and *"smooth* discourse" (with books). And so his little boat rocks in its harbor. There is perhaps more point to this last image than the poet may have intended. Obviously he means it to be a modest and engaging metaphor for his peaceful life far from the madding crowd; but a boat is made to sail, to go somewhere, and, lodged in the harbor always, how is it a boat at all? The poem is an attack on man, not just malicious man or frivolous man, but man involved in a world which necessarily, because it contains love, contains malice and expresses rancor. The poet's best hope is to be barren, without emotion, hope, or aim—as unlike man as possible.

This is too solemn. The poems are trivial and in most obvious senses uncharacteristic. But they do provide a sort of marker for one limit of the range of the poet's vision of ideal man, the other limit of which is marked by his mighty celebration of man, "Earth's paramount Creature," whose unique power it is to converse with eternity. My point is that they are but North and South Poles to one another, belong to the same world, and have much in common. The speaker in this poem shares with metaphysical man the shunning of man's ordinary experience. They have in common their mutual opposition to another sort of man, whose passions and discourse are by no means smooth, who is always talking, having emotions, figuring things out, becoming interested in the accidents of life. Wordsworth does not always seem aware of how sweeping his condemnation of such human experience can be.

Consider the poem called *A Poet's Epitaph:*

Art thou a Statist in the van
Of public conflicts trained and bred?
—First learn to love one living man;
Then may'st thou think upon the dead.

A lawyer art thou?—draw not nigh!
Go, carry to some fitter place
The keenness of that practised eye,
The hardness of that sallow face.

Art thou a Man of purple cheer?
A rosy Man, right plump to see?
Approach; yet, Doctor, not too near,
This grave no cushion is for thee.

Or art thou one of gallant pride,
A Soldier and no man of chaff?
Welcome!—but lay thy sword aside,
And lean upon a peasant's staff.

Physician art thou?—one, all eyes,
Philosopher!—a fingering slave,
One that would peep and botanize
Upon his mother's grave?

Wrapt closely in thy sensual fleece,
O turn aside,—and take, I pray,
That he below may rest in peace,
Thy ever-dwindling soul, away!

A Moralist perchance appears;
Led, Heaven knows how! to this poor sod:
And he has neither eyes nor ears;
Himself his world, and his own God;

One to whose smooth-rubbed soul can cling
Nor form, nor feeling, great or small;
A reasoning, self-sufficing thing,
An intellectual All-in-all!

Shut close the door; press down the latch;
Sleep in thy intellectual crust;
Nor lose ten tickings of thy watch
Near this unprofitable dust.

But who is He, with modest looks,
And clad in homely russet brown?
He murmurs near the running brooks
A music sweeter than their own.

He is retired as noontide dew,
Or fountain in a noon-day grove;
And you must love him, ere to you
He will seem worthy of your love.

The outward shows of sky and earth,
Of hill and valley, he has viewed;
And impulses of deeper birth
Have come to him in solitude.

In common things that round us lie
Some random truths he can impart,—
The harvest of a quiet eye
That broods and sleeps on his own heart.

But he is weak; both Man and Boy,
Hath been an idler in the land;
Contented if he might enjoy
The things which others understand.

—Come hither in thy hour of strength;
Come, weak as is a breaking wave!
Here stretch thy body at full length;
Or build thy house upon this grave.

Wordsworth comes closer here than he ever does anywhere else, if not to the exuberant wit of Pope, at least to the exuberant vituperative energy of Blake, say, or of the Jacobean satirists; and the shift in tone, when he turns his attention to his modest hero, is dazzling. But whom is he attacking? The famous lines are the ones about the philosopher, and they suggest that Wordsworth is attacking the analytical reason of science; certainly he is, and certainly the poem has quite properly been cited most often in that regard. But isn't it more sweeping and comprehensive than it may seem at first? "Are you a doctor, lawyer, soldier, a man in and of the world? Then I know what you are: you are bad." At first we may think he is attacking only those who in their honorable professions deserve to be attacked, the *bad* lawyers, the *bad* doctors, the *bad* politicians. But in the end the poem is only to be understood, the description of its hero only to be explained, if the attack is comprehensively an attack on man's activities in general, his deeds in his world and performance of his ordinary functions.

What is this hero? He is a man defined by his retirement from the world, whose companions are not other men but the brooks near which he murmurs his poems and the "outward shows of sky and earth, / Or hills and valleys," which have expressed for him at times "impulses of deeper birth," themselves the product of his solitude. He is "weak"—apparently both physically and, in the world's sense, intellectually—and he is weak because he has been an "idler," not a physician, moralist, soldier, and because he has been contented to "enjoy" what others "understand." Understanding, then, precludes pleasure, and pleasure understanding; the two are opposites and mutually exclusive. Two extraordinary images sum him up: the truth he knows is the harvest of "a quiet eye / That broods and sleeps on his own heart," and his weakness is the weakness of "a breaking wave." His weakness is his strength: he is a part, an expression, of the sea of infinity which looks like chaos to ordinary men but is the home of profoundest truths; he is borne by his experience as passively as a wave by the sea, and his identity is in the loss of his identity, as a wave declares itself by breaking. His eye is "quiet": he does not see what ordinary men see, but he is satisfied with what would dissatisfy them. And his eye "broods and sleeps on his own heart": his vision takes its rest there, because he is a place of quietness and peace to himself; he is himself the object of his vision, and his vision is like sleep; it is what ordinary men call dreaming, unconsciousness, idleness, but it is true waking and true labor. Nor is his interest in himself like that of the self-regarding moralist, "himself his world," for the poet's self is nature and in his reflection of nature he loses his special individual identity. His egocentricity is as innocent as that of the stock dove brooding over its own sweet voice.[2]

This image of ideal man would lose its point if his opposites were only bad lawyers, bad philosophers, and so forth; the quality of mind of this hero, which is almost mindlessness, would lose much of its point if its antagonist were only the scientific analytical reason. It is more accurate to say that peeping and botanizing are the most concrete instances in the poem of the larger thing it condemns, *all* the ordinary interests of man in his mortal world. The opposition is between the imagination and the "meddling intellect"; but it is larger than that too, or rather, its implications extend almost to the point where we can say the opposition is between the life of man in time and the life of man in eternity. The poem makes some recognition of this in its closing lines, images of the hero's association with the world of death. His characteristic act is to stretch himself out as if in the grave, for his real world is the eternal and his fit companions are the eternally dead.

Behind this poem and all those like it, in other words, is the paradox that he who would save his life must lose it, and the paradox has a very particular and literal, though peculiar, application. This judgment is more subtly apparent in a poem which is a more complete success, though very similar in its manner of expression, the *Lines Written in Early Spring:*

> I heard a thousand blended notes,
> While in a grove I sate reclined,
> In that sweet mood when pleasant thoughts
> Bring sad thoughts to the mind.
>
> To her fair works did Nature link
> The human soul that through me ran;
> And much it grieved my heart to think
> What man has made of man.
>
> Through primrose tufts, in that green bower,
> The periwinkle trailed its wreaths;
> And 'tis my faith that every flower
> Enjoys the air it breathes.
>
> The birds around me hopped and played,
> Their thoughts I cannot measure:—
> But the least motion which they made,
> It seemed a thrill of pleasure.

The budding twigs spread out their fan,
To catch the breezy air;
And I must think, do all I can,
That there was pleasure there.

If this belief from heaven be sent,
If such be Nature's holy plan,
Have I not reason to lament
What man has made of man?

The poem is not more successful than the other one because it makes any kinder or more moderate a judgment on man. Far from it. It is more successful because it knows more clearly how extensive its judgment is, that it includes all men, even the speaker himself, and so we have no room to be confused about its tone. \Nature is the model for man, his exemplar, and its virtue lies in the pleasure it is able to take in its own life, the birds in their motions, the flowers in the air they breathe. The poet can imagine no "thoughts" in natural things, no thinking, but he can imagine enjoyment there. Man is distinguished from nature by his thinking, and his thinking is the equivalent of his inability to take pleasure in his life. It is part of nature's "holy plan" that man should enjoy himself as the flowers and birds do, but he refuses to do so, and the measure of his rebellion is the degree to which he *is* a human being. Man ate of the fruit of knowledge and was expelled from paradise, excluded from his natural kinship to natural things: "The morning shines, / Nor heedeth Man's perverseness." [3] Is the remedy then to lose the power to think? If his thinking is what distinguishes man from nature, and if man was meant to be harmoniously part of nature's plan, then to be truly a man, to be what nature intended, is to be as unlike man in his actuality as possible, to lose man's distinguishing characteristic. Conversely, the poem is brilliantly using the pathetic fallacy to make its point: in taking pleasure in their existence, the things of nature are being better "men" than men are. He who would be truly a man must be as unlike a man as possible. He who would save his life must lose it in nature.

The poem never pretends the problem is more particular, and therefore more capable of solution, than it really is. The satire of *A Poet's Epitaph* is interesting and exciting, but in the end it contributes to a flaw in the poem, for it suggests limitations on the scope of the poet's attack which are not really there. The speaker in the *Epitaph* is as it were a dead man, and thus beyond the range of the attack; the speaker in the *Lines* is still living, therefore himself a part of what he is criticizing. Because he is a man like other men, he is as perversely as they the corrupter of nature's plan, her harmony. And because his perverseness may be defined as the human condition itself, his situation is tragic.

I I

IN SUCH A VIEW of ordinary man, ordinary human relations must be thought of as painful, and especially so because they involve vicissitude and death. In the poem called *The Fountain*,[4] for example, the poet and his old teacher Matthew are together in the countryside one beautiful morning. Matthew, looking at a spring of water before them, draws the sort of contrast we have learned to expect, between the changeless change of the stream, always going yet never gone, and the condition of man, who is aware of change in such a way that he must lament it:

> "No check, no stay, this Streamlet fears;
> How merrily it goes!
> 'Twill murmur on a thousand years,
> And flow as now it flows.
>
> "And here, on this delightful day,
> I cannot choose but think
> How oft, a vigorous man, I lay
> Beside this fountain's brink.
>
> "My eyes are dim with childish tears,
> My heart is idly stirred,
> For the same sound is in my ears
> Which in those days I heard.
>
> "Thus fares it still in our decay:
> And yet the wiser mind
> Mourns less for what age takes away
> Than what it leaves behind.

"The blackbird amid leafy trees,
  The lark above the hill,
Let loose their carols when they please,
  Are quiet when they will.

"With Nature never do *they* wage
  A foolish strife; they see
A happy youth, and their old age
  Is beautiful and free:

"But we are pressed by heavy laws;
  And often, glad no more,
We wear a face of joy, because
  We have been glad of yore."

The "heavy laws" that oppress man are the laws that compel him to feel a sorrow corresponding to the joy his human relationships once gave him, since those relationships are inevitably altered by inconstancy or death. This is also his "foolish strife" against nature, but the poem has no bland assumptions that it would be easy for him to be at one with nature, easy not to be human. Man's folly is indigenous to him. The old man's sorrow for his "kindred laid in earth, / The household hearts that were his own," is unavoidable; but his sorrow that, being human, he must mourn—and that his mourning depends on his previous joy—is much greater: "And yet the wiser mind / Mourns less for what age takes away / Than what it leaves behind." To be at one with nature would be not to be human, so that one would neither have to grieve over bereavement nor experience the anterior joy which causes such grief. The old man is mourning for his humanity.

The point is more simply made in a poem called *The Two April Mornings*,[5] where Matthew describes visiting the grave of his daughter:

"Six feet in earth my Emma lay;
  And yet I loved her more,
For so it seemed, than till that day
  I e'er had loved before.

"And, turning from her grave, I met,
  Beside the churchyard yew,
A blooming Girl, whose hair was wet
  With points of morning dew.

"A basket on her head she bare;
Her brow was smooth and white:
To see a child so very fair,
It was a pure delight!

"No fountain from its rocky cave
E'er tripped with foot so free;
She seemed as happy as a wave
That dances on the sea.

"There came from me a sigh of pain
Which I could ill confine;
I looked at her, and looked again:
And did not wish her mine!"

He does not wish her his, and for the same reasons that, in the other poem, he refuses the poet's offer to be like a son to him. In either case, it would be taking up again the burden of human relationships with their joy and attendant sorrow. And he does not wish her his because the joy her living beauty offers him is as nothing compared to the depth of his relationship to the dead. He loves Emma in her grave more than he had loved her while alive. When he sees the living girl it is as if he were offered a choice between the living and the dead, and he chooses the dead.

For a relationship with the dead is, by that much, more stable than a relationship with the living: the dead are dead and cannot change; though the lover still breathes the giddy air, the beloved is in eternity. This helps explain why so many of the poems of Wordsworth which dramatize human feelings are poems about bereavement. If eternity, changelessness, is the source of truth and its test, then the truth of the feelings of mortal men toward mortal objects is not to be trusted. The farm in *Michael*[6] is a place that seems almost out of time, secluded from the world and its affairs. While he lives there, the boy Luke is like a child of nature. But when he leaves the farm and goes far from his relation to eternal nature, he plays his family false. He does so *inevitably* because when he goes to the city he enters a corrupt, corrupting, and wholly human atmosphere. To live in the mortal world is *by definition* to be fickle.

Consider this beautiful sonnet:

Surprised by joy—impatient as the Wind
I turned to share the transport—Oh! with whom
But Thee, deep buried in the silent tomb,
That spot which no vicissitude can find?
Love, faithful love, recalled thee to my mind—
But how could I forget thee? Through what power,
Even for the least division of an hour,
Have I been so beguiled as to be blind
To my most grievous loss!—That thought's return
Was the worst pang that sorrow ever bore,
Save one, one only, when I stood forlorn,
Knowing my heart's best treasure was no more;
That neither present time, nor years unborn
Could to my sight that heavenly face restore.

We can argue that the sureness and genuineness of the tone here, the absence of the false notes we often hear in dramatic, non-meditative poems of Wordsworth addressed to living people, depends on his daughter being dead. The relationship itself depends on that, is the more real because she is so. What the speaker is distressed about is that he had sometimes forgotten her death, had been able to be "surprised by joy" and so in a sense had been fickle to his grief for her. He was necessarily fickle, because he was still alive and vicissitude is the ordinary human condition. He had been surprised by joy into thinking that his old living relationship with her was still going on, that she was still alive; and this was a kind of unfaithfulness to his realest relationship with her, his grief over her death. The poet grieves that he must, being a living human being, go on having a variety of feelings about things, taking an interest in things.

The ideal relationship, of course, would be the dead speaking to the dead. But it is not possible. Between the living and the dead there is a wall. In *The Affliction of Margaret*,[7] the forlorn mother says:

Perhaps some dungeon hears thee groan,
Maimed, mangled by inhuman men;
Or thou upon a desert thrown
Inheritest the lion's den;
Or hast been summoned to the deep,
Thou, thou and all thy mates, to keep
An incommunicable sleep.

Their "sleep" renders them incommunicado to the living, and there is almost a hint of resentment in the word as she speaks it, for their deaths render him and his mates incommunicado *together*, and perhaps in the world of death to which they have been summoned they speak a language together which human beings cannot understand, from which the mother is excluded. The mother is doubly bereft then, her grief incommunicable to her neighbors, her only relationship being to the uncommunicative dead:

> Beyond participation lie
> My troubles, and beyond relief:
> If any chance to heave a sigh,
> They pity me, and not my grief.
> Then come to me, my Son, or send
> Some tidings that my woes may end;
> I have no other earthly friend!

Human relationships are inevitably painful because one or the other person may die, or because the human heart in its ordinary passions is by definition alterable and not to be trusted; we are constantly, by our human natures, in one way or another bereaving and being bereaved. The relation—or lack of it—between this instability and the ideal human love the poet so passionately wants is illustrated by a poem called *A Complaint:*

> There is a change—and I am poor;
> Your love hath been, nor long ago,
> A fountain at my fond heart's door,
> Whose only business was to flow;
> And flow it did; not taking heed
> Of its own bounty, or my need.
>
> What happy moments did I count!
> Blest was I then all bliss above!
> Now, for that consecrated fount
> Of murmuring, sparkling, living love,
> What have I? Shall I dare to tell?
> A comfortless and hidden well.

A well of love—it may be deep—
I trust it is,—and never dry:
What matter? if the waters sleep
In silence and obscurity.
—Such change, and at the very door
Of my fond heart, hath made me poor.

The poem is uncharacteristic of Wordsworth in that the "living love," the actual relationship between human beings, is not here devaluated in favor of the ideal love. Almost the contrary: the poem asks, what difference does it make if the love, or the possibility of the love, exists and yet is not expressed?

But there is something curious here, which illuminates Wordsworth's notion of the relation between ideal love and its actuality. The ideal, the source, deep in the hidden reaches of the personality, of actual love, is a well which has in the past produced the fountain. For some reason "there is a change," and the water no longer flows forth. But the poem gives no reason why, the images of well and fountain are never developed. The well simply stops producing, yet is supposed to be there still, intact.

The truth is, I think, that the poem cannot carry out its metaphor because it does not express Wordsworth's essential beliefs. It suggests the possibility of success in human relationships, that there is a relation between the sources of love and ordinary human life, and that the love is expressible, as the well is *expressed* by the fountain. But in Wordsworth's more usual view there is no such relation: the only way for human beings successfully to love one another is for them to dwell together in paradise, in eternity, or in their psychological equivalent. A commitment to the arena of chance and change guarantees the failure of human love. Hence the odd truncated quality of a poem which tries to say otherwise.

The most complete parable—though I am not sure it means to be—of the necessary failure of ordinary human relations is the ballad-poem *Ruth*.[8] Again it is a case of the poet setting out to say something which his beliefs about the human situation would not let him say.

Ruth spent her childhood like a Lucy, one of those children who seem but half-human, a child of nature, almost a *thing* of nature. Her mother died when she was an infant, and when her father married again Ruth was neglected, allowed to grow wild.

She "went wandering over dale and hill, / In thoughtless freedom, bold"; and

> . . . she had made a pipe of straw,
> And music from that pipe could draw
> Like sounds of winds and floods;
> Had built a bower upon the green,
> As if she from her birth had been
> An infant of the woods.

She grew up to be wooed and won by a youth whose appearance and life were ominously exotic, like a "panther," like a "dolphin" in the "tropic sea." The tales he told were such tales as "told to any maid / By such a youth, in the green shade, / Were perilous to hear." He promised her a life which would be a sort of paradise, pastoral and with all the charm of the strange and wild:

> He told of girls—a happy rout!
> Who quit their fold with dance and shout,
> Their pleasant Indian town,
> To gather strawberries all day long;
> Returning with a choral song
> When daylight is gone down.
>
> He spake of plants that hourly change
> Their blossoms, through a boundless range
> Of intertwining hues;
> With budding, fading, faded flowers
> They stand the wonder of the bowers
> From morn to evening dews.
>
> He told of the magnolia, spread
> High as a cloud, high over head!
> The cypress and her spire;
> —Of flowers that with one scarlet gleam
> Cover a hundred leagues, and seem
> To set the hills on fire.
>
> The Youth of green savannahs spake,
> And many an endless, endless lake,
> With all its fairy crowds
> Of islands, that together lie
> As quietly as spots of sky
> Among the evening clouds.

So Ruth was seduced by his eloquence to agree to marry him and go away with him to this fabulous America. We have been warned already, by its fairyland trappings, that things are not going to be what she thinks. The youth's voluptuous and languorous environment had made him voluptuous and languorous too, unstable, unfitted to sustain his relationship with her; and so, just as they were about to set sail, he deserted her, and Ruth "could never find him more." She was driven mad by the pain of the betrayal and for three years was pent up in a madhouse; when at last she was released she returned, a vagabond, to the fields and banks of Tone. There her sanity returned, and she became as it were one with the countryside:

> The engines of her pain, the tools
> That shaped her sorrow, rocks and pools,
> And airs that gently stir
> The vernal leaves—she loved them still;
> Nor ever taxed them with the ill
> Which had been done to her.

From this point on, the poem does not seem to know quite what to do with its fable. The life she leads now is "an innocent life," yet "far astray! / And Ruth will, long before her day, / Be broken down and old." So far, nothing else but the logical completion of her misery. But in the end, or in the two stanzas before the last, she becomes a kind of blessed and portentous, almost magical, figure, like the spirit of the countryside:

> That oaten pipe of hers is mute,
> Or thrown away; but with a flute
> Her loneliness she cheers:
> This flute, made of a hemlock stalk,
> At evening in his homeward walk
> The Quantock woodman hears.

> I, too, have passed her on the hills
> Setting her little water-mills
> By spouts and fountains wild—
> Such small machinery as she turned
> Ere she had wept, ere she had mourned,
> A young and happy Child!

On one level, which all signs suggest was the level of intention, the fable is moral and pretty conventionally so, the old story of the smooth-talking drummer come to seduce the innocent country girl. She ought to have known better, she ought to have discerned in his tales of America their elements of fairyland. "America," by this reading, stands for the unreal which it was her mistake to choose, "England" for the real if unglamorous responsibilities and satisfactions of adult life. But the end of the poem suggests another reading, or at least introduces some uncertainties about this one. Ruth is returned to her childhood condition, still wild, still playing her music. Is the poem saying she ought never to have left it, or that in having left it she made a wrong choice? She never "taxed" the rocks and pools, which were the "engines of her pain," with what had happened to her. Were they the engines of her pain in that her acquaintance with natural beauties made the natural beauties of America enticing to her? If so, her marriage was an attempt to prolong her childhood, a refusal to commit herself to the dangers of adult experience. Or were they the engines of her pain in being so much more beautiful than any adult life could have been? By this reading, America is not a false paradise but the actual world in which things are always changing—the flowers budding, fading, faded, the youth always finding new objects to arouse new desire and so bound to be unfaithful. England, then, is not the world of adult responsibility but the paradisal world of her childhood, to which, indulging her, the poem returns her in the end.

I do not see how we can choose with certainty between these two readings, nor how we can avoid the judgment that the poem illustrates how Wordsworth's prevailing despair about the possibilities of ordinary human relationships thwarts his attempt to deal with such experience in moral terms. What is to be learned from experience, if it is better never to have been involved in it?

III

For man living among and submitting to the accidents of time and space, human relations are bound to be painful and even in a certain sense a failure, since they are subject to the corruptions of vicissitude and end inevitably in death. The ideal relationship would be the dead speaking to the dead, but this is not possible.

That is to say, it is not *literally* possible. "Death" means many things in Wordsworth, as we have already seen. It means what it means everywhere else, of course—physical death, the end of human experience and all its possibilities. But it also means to be related to the eternal truths of things and to escape being entangled among their accidents. And in this metaphorical sense it is possible to be "dead" while you are still alive. Or rather, if it is not possible to be "dead" in this way, the accidents of time and space being inescapable, it is possible for the poet to invent a kind of fiction, a mythology of love, in which that which is metaphysical and infinite in every mind relates itself to its counterpart in every other, the deep calling to the deep. Thus in the poem *Louisa,* which is a sort of love song, the object of the speaker's love becomes almost a supernatural figure:

> I met Louisa in the shade,
> And, having seen that lovely Maid,
> Why should I fear to say
> That, nymph-like, she is fleet and strong,
> And down the rocks can leap along
> Like rivulets in May?
>
> And she hath smiles to earth unknown;
> Smiles, that with motion of their own
> Do spread, and sink, and rise;
> That come and go with endless play,
> And ever, as they pass away,
> Are hidden in her eyes.
>
> She loves her fire, her cottage-home;
> Yet o'er the moorland will she roam
> In weather rough and bleak;
> And, when against the wind she strains,
> Oh! might I kiss the mountain rains
> That sparkle on her cheek.
>
> Take all that's mine "beneath the moon,"
> If I with her but half a noon
> May sit beneath the walls
> Of some old cave, or mossy nook,
> When up she winds along the brook
> To hunt the waterfalls.

She is enough like a thing of nature to figure as one of its spirits, "nymph-like" as she leaps along like "rivulets in May." What the speaker responds to in her is this association with nature—he wants to kiss "the mountain rains / That sparkle on her cheek"—and more than that, he responds to the suggestion that she is more properly a thing of the other nature behind the natural scene. She has "smiles to earth unknown," smiles which are meanings in themselves, almost without reference to her physical self, "with motion of their own," and which have their own secrecy and elusiveness, hiding themselves in her eyes. She is an actual girl, of course, who "loves her fire and cottage-home." (Else what point would the fiction about her have? She is heaven on earth.) And the speaker knows that his ideal perception of her cannot last, for he is a human being and so is she: there is a kind of wistfulness about "If I with her but half a noon / May sit beneath the walls." Deep can call to deep only fitfully, and their intercourse is at the mercy of time.

The same fusion of uncertainty and exaltation invests a poem which was originally intended as part of this one, *To a Young Lady:*

> Dear Child of Nature, let them rail!
> —There is a nest in a green dale,
> A harbour and a hold;
> Where thou, a Wife and Friend, shalt see
> Thy own heart-stirring days, and be
> A light to young and old.
>
> There, healthy as a shepherd boy,
> And treading among flowers of joy
> Which at no season fade,
> Thou, while thy babes around thee cling,
> Shalt show us how divine a thing
> A Woman may be made.
>
> Thy thoughts and feelings shall not die,
> Nor leave thee, when grey hairs are nigh,
> A melancholy slave;
> But an old age serene and bright,
> And lovely as a Lapland night,
> Shall lead thee to thy grave.

The young lady, according to the subtitle, "had been reproached for taking long walks in the country"; the poem probably takes its occasion from an actual rebuke. And it holds a beautiful and precarious balance between addressing her as an actual young lady and as a divine thing. It even asserts, at the end of stanza two, that a sort of divinity can be fashioned out of ordinary experience, by contact with nature, but in this case even this nature is a fiction, in which she is transformed into a shepherd boy, "treading among flowers of joy / Which at no season fade." The poem is aware of its own artificiality and knows that it is not true to the facts. The metaphors of nature as a "nest," a "harbour," and a "hold" suggest this awareness, for they are metaphors of protection from the vicissitudes which are the facts of life. And the awareness is most moving in the simile with which the poem closes: "But an old age serene and bright, / And lovely as a Lapland night, / Shall lead thee to thy grave." Not only as lovely as a Lapland night, but as exotic, as foreign to our ordinary experience of old age.

The poem is probably not ironic in any self-destructive sense. In one way the speaker really believes that she can so respond to the temporal scene that it will be changed for her into a landscape where no flowers fade, and she will be changed with it into a divine creature indomitable against the terrors of vicissitude; but in another way he knows that what he is promising her is as impossible to realize as a Lapland night.

The special quality of *She dwelt among the untrodden ways,* one of the most famous of the lyrics, depends upon the complex feeling that the girl is at once victim and goddess:

> She dwelt among the untrodden ways
>   Beside the springs of Dove,
> A Maid whom there were none to praise
>   And very few to love.
>
> A violet by a mossy stone
>   Half hidden from the eye!
> —Fair as a star, when only one
>   Is shining in the sky.

> She lived unknown, and few could know
> When Lucy ceased to be;
> But she is in her grave, and, oh,
> The difference to me!

The two attitudes of the speaker toward her are expressed, and expressed as equals, in every line. She dwelt among the "untrodden ways," was a maiden whom there were "none to praise, / And very few to love," was a "violet" "half hidden from the eye," and fair as a star "when only one / Is shining in the sky." She was all these things because she was only a humble country girl, and nothing remarkable in herself—from the world's point of view—and she was all these things because only a poet like this speaker was wise enough in the truth of nature to love her and to know what she stood for. That she was a violet says not only that she was humble and pretty enough, but that she was one with nature, that she had achieved the ideal human condition of being hardly human at all. She had become part of that serene order which human beings ordinarily cannot know, and which even this speaker can know only imperfectly. This is what saves the closing line from being sentimental, for when she died she denied the factual possibility of human beings being part of that natural order—violets do not die in the sense that human beings do—and at the same time her death was a sign that he could not sustain the eternality he discerned in her. It was his vision of unity that died, as for a mortal it must.

This same pattern, though more elaborately and fully expressed, characterizes another of the "Lucy" poems, *Three years she grew in sun and shower:*

> Three years she grew in sun and shower,
> Then Nature said, "A lovelier flower
> On earth was never sown;
> This Child I to myself will take;
> She shall be mine, and I will make
> A Lady of my own.
>
> "Myself will to my darling be
> Both law and impulse: and with me
> The Girl, in rock and plain,

In earth and heaven, in glade and bower,
Shall feel an overseeing power
To kindle or restrain.

"She shall be sportive as the fawn
That wild with glee across the lawn
Or up the mountain springs;
And her's shall be the breathing balm,
And her's the silence and the calm
Of mute insensate things.

"The floating clouds their state shall lend
To her; for her the willow bend;
Nor shall she fail to see
Even in the motions of the Storm
Grace that shall mould the Maiden's form
By silent sympathy.

"The stars of midnight shall be dear
To her; and she shall lean her ear
In many a secret place
Where rivulets dance their wayward round,
And beauty born of murmuring sound
Shall pass into her face.

"And vital feelings of delight
Shall rear her form to stately height,
Her virgin bosom swell;
Such thoughts to Lucy I will give
While she and I together live
Here in this happy dell."

Thus Nature spake—The work was done—
How soon my Lucy's race was run!
She died, and left to me
This heath, this calm, and quiet scene;
The memory of what has been,
And never more will be.

Nature is his successful rival for the hand of Lucy. The things
that made her beautiful and pleasing to him, the wildness of a
fawn, the special sympathy of her grace with the clouds, the

willows, the stars, the murmuring streams, are actually the work of that nature which is going to take his Lucy away from him. We are made to feel two exactly contradictory feelings: first, that it is a pity so beautiful a girl should have been taken away so young, just when she had been perfected for her life on earth; and second, that her death is justified and right, the only adequate culmination of the work Nature was doing. Even in her life on earth she was in a special communication with natural things, and before our eyes she becomes not so much a human being as a sort of compendium of nature:

> "The stars of midnight shall be dear
> To her; and she shall lean her ear
> In many a secret place
> Where rivulets dance their wayward round,
> And beauty born of murmuring sound
> Shall pass into her face.

The "calm" and "silence" Lucy knows so well are not what the speaker comes to know, for his is the "calm and quiet scene" of his bereavement, of having been left behind, and hers is the calm of a communion with nature which is the presagement, and finally the equivalent, of her own death. Yet perhaps the calm he comes to know depends on her death and is a positive value he has derived from it. We are asked to feel at once the pathos of the physical death (and the grief of the bereaved) and at the same time the rightness of it. For she has not "really died," she has only gone away to live forever with immortal nature; there is no place within the limits of human mortality for her mystical identification with nature; the poet is left behind with his understanding, that second-best, the symbolic imagination.

All this brings us to the lyric which is at the powerful center of this poet's art, *A slumber did my spirit seal:*

> A slumber did my spirit seal;
>   I had no human fears:
> She seemed a thing that could not feel
>   The touch of earthly years.

No motion has she now, no force;
    She neither hears nor sees;
Rolled round in earth's diurnal course,
    With rocks, and stones, and trees.

The poem is difficult almost by reason of its apparent simplicity, which nearly prevents us from lookng beyond the immediate impression of grief to the unsentimental sources of the grief's extraordinary power. One is inclined to say, "He loved her so much that he could not imagine that she could die," and let it go at that, content to marvel. But the poem is too complex for such mere admiration. In the first stanza the poet says that while she was alive he himself was asleep, perhaps even dead, to her vitality. Though his love was great it was imperceptive, and it was inadequate in that it failed to grant her the dignity of her human mortality. He idealized her to the degree that he put her beyond the ordinary processes of nature, and had "no human fears" that she was in any way involved in change and death. In the second stanza his sleepy imperceptiveness gets its reward: he "awakens" to discover that she has now in fact been put beyond humanity and the processes of nature (as they apply to living human beings), for she is now in fact dead. She is, to be sure, intimately involved with those processes, but in a new way. The poem has the structure of a very serious joke: the poet gets exactly what he bargained for, shockingly and in an unexpected form. She is now a "thing" indeed, can now indeed not feel the touch "of earthly years," is now in a dreadfully exact sense inhuman, for she has become merely another element of unhuman nature, rolled round with "rocks, and stones, and trees."

One could work for pages among the suggestions of words like "seal," "force," "diurnal course," "rocks," and "stones," but for our purpose the main point is already clear. The poem is saying beautifully something about the insensitiveness of one human being to the death, and consequently to the life, in another. (The full stop after "human fears" even suggests that his imperceptiveness proceeded from some kind of unhumanness in himself.) If the poet could have seen that she would necessarily alter and die, if he had not put her beyond nature and so made a "thing" of her, he might have been able to value her properly. Now that she has in fact become a "thing" and is in fact—though in an ironical sense—a part of nature, he is at last, too late, awake to her humanity.

One is tempted to protest against this reading so far by saying it destroys the effect of the poem as a love poem. The first stanza undoubtedly *is* describing the magnitude of his love. Nevertheless the poem also says the love ought to have been accompanied by a realistic awareness of the girl's limitations in mortality, and that to rebuke himself for not having believed she was mortal and would die is actually a very great compliment—her *only* limitation was death. Also, we have not yet accounted for the most powerful effect of all, which arises from the poet's realization that death has taken her *regardless* of his own errors of insight, and will keep her *regardless* of his new awareness of her mortality. This is the last twist of the joke: even to have gone on "sleeping," to have gone on idealizing her in his fashion, might have been better than to have lost her so irrecoverably. Thus, though the life and death in her ought to have been meaningful to him in one way, the unchangeable calamity of her death renders all such considerations in another way meaningless.

This is an attitude toward mortality which recognizes and accepts its inevitable power, and yet accepts it not fatuously, blandly, nor gladly, but with a full realization of the pain that change involves for human beings. The poem is a marvelous demonstration of the "sense of reality" Mr. Trilling talks about,[9] the acceptance of time and space which is the cause and best resource of the symbolic imagination.

But there is more to be said. How can we explain the grandeur of the concluding lines—"Rolled round in earth's diurnal course, / With rocks, and stones, and trees"—except by saying that there is a countercurrent in the poem, made more impressive by the power of what it denies? Her death was right, after all, for by dying she was one with the natural processes that made her die, and fantastically ennobled thereby. The poem is a distillation of *Three years she grew.* Eternal nature is her true lover, and the poet's first idealization of her was right after all, for she had nothing to do with humanity or mortality, and her true relation was to the world of eternity, from which he is excluded. It is better after all to become immortal than to be the mortal object of a human relationship, however beautiful.

These poems are not only beautiful in themselves, but paradigms for the poet's imaginative experience of the world. These girls, half-goddesses though also wholly human, are his chief, or perhaps his most successful, symbols for the relation with the eternal which he is always seeking. They are natural emanations of the landscape, creatures of the temporal scene, but their humanness, the fact that they are girls and not flowers, means they are the fulfillment of his promise to himself that man and nature can be one, that man can be as harmoniously a part of the eternal process of things as flowers are, which die but die without complaint. In one way or another, the speaker is uncertain of his vision of these girls; or rather, he is certain of the instability and perishability of his vision of them. He knows he is making up a fiction and that his fiction will not be able to sustain itself forever. This is one way of reading their deaths. But there is another. They die also because death is the natural culmination of what they have been developing toward. They are distinguished from ordinary human beings, from the speaker who declares his love for them, by the extraordinary completeness of their relation to eternal nature, and they die only to go home where they belong. Their relation to the metaphysical reality is mystical, as his, governed by the laws of time and change, is but sacramental. That is why he is always their unsuccessful lover. These poems are at once among Wordsworth's proudest celebrations of the poet, who alone evaluates properly what he sees, and among his most moving acknowledgments that the poetic imagination is not the highest. The "imagination" of these girls is the highest, for it exists in their being, not in any exercise of the mind nor in any *activity* at all.

It is the poet's imagination which is finally the subject matter of these poems. The poetic imagination discovers in the world symbols which stand for and are the relation of time to eternity. The success of the imagination is thus great. But its failure is correspondingly great, and inevitable. A symbol is by definition perishable, and so is the eye that sees it. And there is another success and corresponding failure. A symbol may by the agency of its temporal part eventually fail, but while it is a success it is an image not only of the present relation between the finite and the infinite, but also a nostalgic evocation of the total—not symbolic but mystical—identity with eternity which the poet feels he once possessed. It is then at once a prophecy of that identification and a sad emblem to the poet of what he regards as the failure of his life, his own exclusion from that identification. A sad emblem of his rage against life itself, against the limits of mortality.

IV

BUT WE SAID EARLIER that the "man" the love of nature leads us to love is one of two antithetical heroes—the hero of the sacramental imagination, the poet; and the hero of the mystical imagination, who cannot be so easily characterized, and who is apparent in the verse in a number of forms which define a tendency, sometimes very plain and clear, other times quite obscure and difficult to discern. The tendency is present in the "Lucy" poems, of course, in the sense that what the speaker is contemplating there is the image of a perfect relation with eternity of which he himself is incapable, and he laments his incapability at least as strongly as he laments the physical deaths of the girls. They died of their mysticism; or their mysticism was itself a kind of "death" anyway, of which their physical deaths were only the most concrete expressions.

But one wants to know more about such figures, and about their implications for the poet's view of ordinary human life. To find out more about them it is necessary to look at a number of poems which deal with them less covertly, more explicitly. The first, and by far the most important of these, are the poems which deal with children.

The key signature of these poems is *My heart leaps up*:

> My heart leaps up when I behold
>   A rainbow in the sky:
> So was it when my life began;
> So is it now I am a man;
> So be it when I shall grow old,
>   Or let me die!

> The Child is father of the Man;
> And I could wish my days to be
> Bound each to each by natural piety.

At its simplest, the poem recommends that we remain childlike at heart, that our every perception be "descended" from our childish perceptions, as their children. To be childlike apparently has something to do with being responsive to the natural scene, and nature apparently means the immediate and superficial attraction of a scene, but also, as we have learned to expect by now, the harmony and continuity of natural things in their relations with one another, storm followed by sunshine, rain by rainbow.

The beginning of the poem seems confident that the speaker is perfectly responsive to nature, successful in his natural piety; the end is a little less certain and sure of itself—"And I *could wish* my days to be / Bound each to each by natural piety." Natural piety is no easy thing. The phrase itself suggests some of the difficulties: though it may simply mean that piety which "comes naturally" and easily from the heart, or perhaps a simple pleasure in nature which is comparable to worship, it may also mean a piety toward the abiding in things, their continuity, which is learned from and is the human counterpart of the piety they themselves demonstrate in their harmonious round. It is hard for a human being to be like nature, and the poem knows it.

The famous line about the child being the father of the man expresses a feeling about childhood which is beautiful and impressive, but troubling too. As it is better to be a father than a child—one is wiser in adulthood, more knowledgeable, less helpless—then to grow up is to grow less wise, less knowledgeable, more helpless. As it is better to be a child than a man—one is more innocent in childhood, less distracted and corrupted by experience, closer to the sources of truth—then to grow up is to be corrupted, further from the truth, less innocent. The cards are stacked. The line *appears* to be saying something about a desirable way to develop, but it really expresses an antagonism to development itself: however you look at it, the worst thing that can happen is to grow up. The sober cheer which, at first hearing, is the dominant tone of the poem, is thus thwarted and denied by these implications of the lines, and denied in a way we cannot very confidently ascribe to the poet's intention.

This little poem expresses in a kind of shorthand almost all the elements of Wordsworth's attitudes toward childhood, but to understand them better we need to look at some poems which will give us a characteristic vocabulary to examine, a vocabulary Wordsworth was accustomed to use about childhood.

First of all, the poem called *To H. C.*:

> O Thou! whose fancies from afar are brought;
> Who of they words dost make a mock apparel,
> And fittest to unutterable thought
> The breeze-like motion and the self-born carol;
> Thou faery voyager! that dost float
> In such clear water, that thy boat
> May rather seem
> To brood on air than on an earthly stream;
> Suspended in a stream as clear as sky,
> Where earth and heaven do make one imagery;
> O blessed vision! happy child!
> Thou art so exquisitely wild,
> I think of thee with many fears
> For what may be thy lot in future years.
>
> I thought of times when Pain might be thy guest,
> Lord of thy house and hospitality;
> And Grief, uneasy lover! never rest
> But when she sate within the touch of thee.
> O too industrious folly!
> O vain and causeless melancholy!
> Nature will either end thee quite;
> Or, lengthening out thy season of delight,
> Preserve for thee, by individual right,
> A young lamb's heart among the full-grown flocks.
> What hast thou to do with sorrow,
> Or the injuries of to-morrow?
> Thou art a dew-drop, which the morn brings forth,
> Ill-fitted to sustain unkindly shocks,
> Or to be trailed along the soiling earth;
> A gem that glitters while it lives,
> And no forewarning gives!
> But, at the touch of wrong, without a strife,
> Slips in a moment out of life.

The child has brought its fancies "from afar." Its language is only a kind of "mock apparel"; its expression of its knowledge is in its *being*, not in its *saying*, and in its essential and stripped being, "fittest to unutterable thought" whose nature is "breeze-like" and as if from the faery world. The child is poised in a familiar Wordsworthian scene, in a boat on a quiet stream whose waters reflect the sky so perfectly that the two, earth and heaven, seem one. It is the child in the center of this scene who reconciles the heaven and earth which, in our adult experience, so reasonable and expressible, are seen as fundamentally disparate, even hostile.

The child is "exquisitely wild," foreign to our adult experience and unrestricted by our adult limitations. But the poem is a lament; the child is after all six years old and on the verge of that rationality and self-consciousness which will destroy its "childness," its wildness, its special powers of reconciliation. The poet looks forward with fear to the time when pain will be Hartley Coleridge's guest, when he will willfully and of his own perverse adult accord invite pain into the house of himself. Then his only lover will be grief. This will be the end of the child in him, unless, by some miraculous caprice of nature, his season of delight will be preserved and he will continue to be a lamb "among the full-grown flocks." The poem does not take this alternative very seriously, of course, for it returns to imagery which suggests the irrevocable impermanence and instability of the child's state. Hartley is a "dew-drop," which has only to do with the morning and at the touch of wrong will slip "in a moment out of life."

Does this mean he will die easily, that a child is more vulnerable to physical death than we are? Or does it mean that adulthood, maturity, is a kind of death? Both at once. There are complex changes and interchanges of attitude towards "life" and "death" here. In one sense, "life" means that special status of unutterable knowledge and accord with the divine in things, which the first stanza described, and "death" then means the loss of that accord, the growth of the lamb into a full-grown sheep. In another sense, the child is in some special relation to the world of eternity, which is from our mortal point of view a world of "death," beyond the limits of our lives. The maturing of the child is only the measure of its distance from that world, so that the line could be reasonably construed as "slips in a moment *into* life" without changing the feelings involved in it at all. The child is distinguished from us by his aliveness, by the "breeze-like motion and the self-born carol," but he gets this virtue from his closeness to heaven, or from being hardly actual, a "faery" figure, a "blessed vision." He will grow out of this special virtue, away from that "heaven" which is the world of eternity. And this growing up will be a sort of death, slipping in a moment out of the only life that matters.

Almost no poem about children is free from this paradox of life and death. In *We are seven*,[10] for example, the paradox is almost the formal cause of the poem. The opening stanza is heavy with a tender and indulgent sense of superiority and knowledgeablility in the adult speaking to other adults about a little child:

> A simple Child,
> That lightly draws its breath,
> And feels its life in every limb,
> What should it know of death?

It is as if the adult were saying: "How can we expect her, a mere child, to understand such things, which *we* understand as a matter of course?" But as a child, she is distinguished from adults by feeling her life "in every limb." Our adult knowledge, then, may be defined as the loss of that feeling, or of that power of total feeling—a loss of the knowledge, which children have, of the only life that matters.

The poem exhibits this kind of irony throughout, making us read it two ways at once, either to show the obstinate naïveté of the child, who refuses to understand that her brother and sister are really dead, or to emphasize the obstinate sophistication of the speaker, who refuses to recognize the superiority of the child's wisdom. For she knows that there is an unbroken continuity between living and dead, which makes it possible for her to sit beside their graves and sing to them. She can sing to them and share her life with them because they are now a part of eternal nature, which is the true life—and so, being a child, is she.

The chief beauty of the poem arises from the naturalistic accuracy with which it makes its point. We really do feel that the child is naïve and unable to understand the facts of life—or rather of death—at the same time that we take pleasure in the way the speaker is confounded by her. The fact of physical death is incontrovertible. We, and the speaker, know this, and the child really *is* ignorant in refusing to face it. But her real ignorance equals a real wisdom, for she knows about eternal life in a way that we, being adults, cannot know about it.

The poem manipulates our social feelings to make its point, too. This is a "rustic, woodland" girl, and "wildly clad." Her ignorance depends on this as well. The poet and his audience are allied in their relative urbanity, then, and the child's failure to understand death is partly the fault of her bumpkin rudeness. But this fosters an irony too, for the poet and the reader he associates with himself are then the immemorial city slicker, whose smart-aleck city knowledge is put to rout by country innocence.

And the child's wildness is more than rusticity. It is the wildness also of H. C., of the child untamed by mortality, wild because alien to our limited world, as if children were creatures from another sphere, possessing another sort of knowledge. Their wildness is their relation to another sort of nature than adults can know.

This pattern is very plain in the ballad-poem *Lucy Gray*,[11] which is too long and familiar to quote in full. Lucy is described by images of wild and innocent animals—the fawn, the hare, the roe—and associated with the sweet unconscious growth of natural things; she is the "sweetest thing that ever grew / Beside a human door!" One day her father asked her to go to town, to carry a lantern to light her mother's way home through the snow. She went willingly, as blithe as "the mountain roe." But she never reached the town. Her parents searched for her everywhere and found her nowhere, but the next morning they found her footprints, which led to the middle of a bridge and disappeared.

The poem is founded on a true story Wordsworth's sister told him. The actual child's footsteps

> were traced by her parents to the middle of the lock of a canal, and no other vestige of her, backward or forward, could be traced. The body however was found in the canal.[12]

Wordsworth goes on to say:

The way in which the incident was treated and the spiritualizing of the character might furnish hints for contrasting the imaginative influences which I have endeavoured to throw over common life with Crabbe's matter of fact style of treating subjects of the same kind.

There is really no other way to understand "spiritualizing" and "imaginative influences" than as referring to the suggestion in the poem that she may not after all have "died" in the ordinary sense, but may have been translated into an identification with immortal nature. The "point" of *Lucy Gray* seems to be that a child is at once specially vulnerable to physical death and specially impervious to it. She disappears in a storm, but no corpse is ever "found in the canal." She may still be a "living child," and may still be seen as she sings a "solitary song / That whistles in the wind."

The speaker takes no overt position about this, recounting the legend of her immortality fairly dispassionately:

> —Yet some maintain that to this day
> She is a living child;
> That you may see sweet Lucy Gray
> Upon the lonesome wild.

But the rhyme words here are identical with those of the first stanza, as if to remind us of them, and the poet may be hinting that he believes the legend and has proof of its truth:

> Oft I had heard of Lucy Gray:
> And, when I crossed the wild,
> I chanced to see at break of day
> The solitary child.

She has, in every adult sense, died. But the snow into which she disappeared was as a curtain through which she passed into a world in which she is more at home than she ever could have been in the mortal world. She has exchanged human "life" for a life of another kind, a life which is really life, but which adult human beings can only define as death.

Again, the chief strength of the poem derives from the justice it accords both views of things. If Lucy is the most attractive figure in the poem, wild and innocent as she is, and if lines like "the sweetest thing that ever grew / Beside a human door!" suggest that she was too good for human life, the father is an adequate counterbalancing figure of adult responsibility, and Lucy's death occurs, in one sense, because she was only an irresponsible child. She dies, as it were, of an access of merriness; her "wanton" feet carried her out of this world, in a game of metaphysical hide-and-seek with her "wretched parents." Our pity on this level of the poem is for the parents, bewildered as they are by the playfulness of the metaphysical child, the changeling they had given birth to.

Consider finally *There was a Boy*, which was later incorporated into *The Prelude*, but also was printed during the poet's lifetime as a separate poem and carried as the first of the "Poems of the Imagination":

> There was a Boy; ye knew him well, ye cliffs
> And islands of Winander!—many a time,
> At evening, when the earliest stars began
> To move along the edges of the hills,
> Rising or setting, would he stand alone,
> Beneath the trees, or by the glimmering lake;
> And there, with fingers interwoven, both hands
> Pressed closely palm to palm and to his mouth
> Uplifted, he, as through an instrument,
> Blew mimic hootings to the silent owls,
> That they might answer him.—And they would shout
> Across the watery vale, and shout again,
> Responsive to his call,—with quivering peals,
> And long halloos, and screams, and echoes loud
> Redoubled and redoubled; concourse wild
> Of jocund din! And, when there came a pause
> Of silence such as baffled his best skill:
> Then, sometimes, in that silence, while he hung
> Listening, a gentle shock of mild surprise
> Has carried far into his heart the voice
> Of mountain-torrents; or the visible scene
> Would enter unawares into his mind
> With all its solemn imagery, its rocks,
> Its woods, and that uncertain heaven received
> Into the bosom of the steady lake.

> This boy was taken from his mates, and died
> In childhood, ere he was full twelve years old.
> Pre-eminent in beauty is the vale
> Where he was born and bred: the church-yard hangs
> Upon a slope above the village-school;
> And, through that churchyard when my way has led
> On summer-evenings, I believe, that there
> A long half-hour together I have stood
> Mute—looking at the grave in which he lies!

In a passage (later deleted) in the preface to the 1815 edition,
Wordsworth says this of the poem:

> I dismiss this subject with observing—that, in the series of
> Poems placed under the head of Imagination, I have begun with
> one of the earliest processes of Nature in the development of this fac-
> ulty. Guided by one of my own primary consciousnesses, I have
> presented a commutation and transfer of internal feelings, co-
> operating with external accidents, to plant, for immortality, images
> of sound and sight, in the celestial soil of the Imagination. The
> Boy, there introduced, is listening, with something of a feverish
> and restless anxiety, for the recurrence of those riotous sounds
> which he had previously excited; and, at the moment when the
> intenseness of his mind is beginning to remit, he is surprised into
> a perception of the solemn and tranquillizing images which the
> Poem describes.[13]

This is a sufficiently plain account of the first paragraph of the
poem, and it is easy to understand from it why the poem was
placed first in its category. It demonstrates the saving powers of
the childhood imagination, which identifies itself with the universe while at the same time it is unaware of what it has done. It
is thus one of the primary consciousnesses of which we are really
*un*conscious, but which serve as "fountain-lights" for the later
experiences of the adult symbolic or sacramental imagination, itself necessarily aware and conscious of what is happening. We
could even say that this boy's transactions with eternity are neither
one nor the other, neither mystical nor sacramental, but both,
for though his perception is "unawares" it is a perception which
uses the images of the temporal scene. The passage is then the
most hopeful we have yet read about the development of adequate

adult imaginative powers; the boy is at the end of childhood, preparing to enter maturity, and is learning, so to speak, to be a poet.

But he dies. Is not his death perhaps a metaphor for the poet's despair about the possibility of such a development? The mystical imagination dies with childhood, and the poet's account of the poem claims that the boy's death may symbolize the same doubts about the vital continuity between the childhood and adult imaginations which we saw expressed in the great ode. We can say, of course, what we said about the deaths in the other poems— that for the boy to die was the natural culmination of his imaginative act. He was commuted and transformed into the nature he responded to, and nature commuted and transformed into him. The two participated in a perfect and equal exchange. He became his universe, and if the "immortality" for which the sounds and sights of our mortal world are planted in "celestial soil" means eternal life, it also means, from the point of view of our mortal adult limitations, a kind of death. But it works the other way too, and does so *necessarily*. To the degree that his death is the sign of the success of his childhood imaginative act, it is the sign also of the necessary failure of his imagination when grown up. The one depends on the other.

To be a child, in these poems, is to be wild—to be innocent, inarticulate, and wise in the relation of time to eternity, and to be so not by any process of conscious thought but in one's state of being, like H. C. suspended between heaven and earth, like Lucy Gray so wantonly wandering into the other world, her true home. Above all, it is to be uncommitted to the world of adult experience, this limited world of time and space, as the little girl in *We are seven* is uncommitted by her very ignorance of its ways, as Lucy and the Winander Boy are uncommitted by their deaths, and Hartley Coleridge by his fragility and vulnerability to death. It begins to be clear that these children are Wordsworth's formulation for a state of being which resists and refuses the involvements incumbent on us as adult mortals, and which is therefore the more beautiful and admirable—in Wordsworth's view. They are the purest instances of heroes of the mystical imagination, of the union of time and eternity, and they are so because they have so little of time, of the finite, about them.

If we argue that Wordsworth "really believed" all this to be true of children, we may be right. There is no telling what he "really believed" in such cases, or how literally he took what he said. But it is safer, and more profitable, to think of them as symbols for a state of mind or of being which he knew—the poems say over and over again that he knew—to be in fact impossible for himself or for any adult human being, but which he desired passionately. Indeed, we can almost say that the *only* passion—or a passion so powerful and overriding as to seem unchallenged—which his most characteristic poems convincingly display is the passion for such a state of being. These children are, as it were, a fiction which idealizes and makes beautiful the same antipathy which we saw in much cruder forms in *Personal Talk*. It seems to me impossible and unnecessary to discover whether the fiction came from the antipathy or the antipathy from the fiction, whether he was first ideologically convinced in his views of human experience or whether the ideology was the product of a sensibility which by some warp or by some psychological or physiological hurt had been conditioned to respond to the world the way it did.

The word "fiction" is dangerous here anyway. A poem like *A slumber did my spirit seal* is evidence enough that Wordsworth knew he was dealing in a fiction—almost a private mythology, complete with a goddess—but he could not give up his fiction just because he realized it was one; it is nevertheless more real to him than "actuality," than *anybody's* collection of mere data. Actuality has reality for him as the motive for inventing his fiction: a fiction in this sense is nothing more nor less than an interpretation of actuality, so that it becomes for the interpreter his *reality*, and in this Wordsworth is no different from the rest of us except in the degree of his powers But even this is not *quite* true. Reality for any man must be his own peculiar distortion of the "objective data" of the world, and in this way every man has his fiction of things, which is his reality or the habit of his mind. But the degree of distortion (the common reader, the "ordinary man," being our measuring instrument) is not usually so great, nor its relation to its actuality so hostile to it, as it appears to be in Wordsworth. It is not necessary to think therefore that in any simple way Wordsworth falsified, prettified, or "romanticized" his native region. Such terms are too simply invidious, and they suggest at best a frivolity and at worst a self-deception of a sort of which Wordsworth could not possibly have been guilty. His work is inimical to the kind of pastoral one associates with such prettification or falsification. But it is also in a serious but highly unusual sense a version of pastoral.

I suppose the most obvious appeal of the conventional pastoral mode was that it showed to people of many responsibilities and involvements images of a remarkable freedom, and to people of many conflicts images of a remarkable harmony. Dr. Johnson, in the thirty-sixth *Rambler*, "Delights of Pastoral Poetry," says it best:

> There is scarcely any species of poetry that has allured more readers or excited more writers than the Pastoral. It is generally pleasing because it entertains the mind with representations of scenes familiar to almost every imagination, and of which all can equally judge whether they are well described. It exhibits a life to which we have always been accustomed to associate peace and leisure and innocence; and therefore we readily set open the heart for the admission of its images, which contribute to drive away cares and perturbations, and suffer ourselves, without resistance, to be transported to Elysian regions, where we are to meet with nothing but joy and plenty and contentment; where every gale whispers pleasure and every shade promises repose.[14]

"Peace" and "innocence" are certainly characteristics of Wordsworth's pastoral regions, and one of their functions is surely to drive away cares and perturbations and fill us with joy and contentment. There are differences, of course. Wordsworth's regions are not Elysian nor Sicilian nor Arcadian, but English, with English place names; his pastoral figures sometimes really labor and are frequently in trouble; and this lends to his pastoral fiction an air of naturalism which is in many ways misleading.

But there is a more important difference. Again Johnson is helpful, when he says:

> Not only the images of rural life, but the occasions on which they can be properly produced, are few and general. The state of a man confined to the employments and pleasures of the country is so little diversified, and exposed to so few of those accidents which produce perplexities, terrors, and surprises in more

complicated transactions, that he can be shown but seldom in such circumstances as attract curiosity. His ambition is without policy, and his love without intrigue. He has no complaint to make of his rival but that he is richer than himself, nor any disasters to lament but a cruel mistress or a bad harvest.[15]

The urban life may seem to be condemned here for its intrigue, its "policy," its profusion of complaint, terror, perplexity, and surprise. But Johnson is not so much comparing a "bad" world to a "good" one as he is contrasting the real world to a simplified and idealized fiction. So his commentary is finally invidious to the world of pastoral. The world of actuality is more interesting than the Arcadian groves, in the end. If it involves more terrors and perplexities, it involves also more of the obligations and commitments which define human experience. Johnson's vocabulary about the differences between city and country is in some ways not unlike Wordsworth's, but its connotations are all different. Johnson chooses the city, Wordsworth chooses the country: the country is less "diversified" in its employments and pleasures; its images are "few and general"; it has less "complicated transactions."

William Empson's general definition of pastoral is useful here too: pastoral is a "double attitude . . . of the complex man to the simple one," which produces the formula: " 'I am in one way better, in another not so good.' "[16] It is in the relations between simple and complex that the formula is helpful for studying Wordsworth, and not always because he fits it. Certainly in some cases he does, as in *A slumber did my spirit seal*, where the speaker, bound in the entangling complexities of his mortal nature, gives his admiration to a girl who is simpler than he because she is free of those trammels. He is in one way "better" than she is, because he is aware of his moral responsibility to recognize the limits of mortality; he is "not so good" because she *needs* no such responsibility or awareness. But even here the balance is not quite kept, for the final triumph is hers.

Wordsworth's evaluation is usually more openly in favor of the "simple," and in this respect he differs most from what we usually think of as "pastoral." The pastoral poem is, in our ordinary view of it, written from the standpoint of the complex "urban" mind, and though the pastoral scene and its characters may act as a sort of criticism, sometimes a very serious one, of the complex urban life, still the poet's loyalty is to that life, if only because he knows that it has to be. What good is a criticism unless you value what is being criticized? In Wordsworth's pastoral, the poet is involved in complexities and cannot escape them, and usually knows it, but his emotional commitment is all to the simple, to the fiction which criticizes the actual.

What does "simple" mean here? It means everything that childhood meant in the poems we have been looking at. And it has other embodiments too, old men, and idiots, and above all Wordsworth's ideal peasants, with their immediate relation to the permanent and awful forms of nature. The appeal of the humble and rustic to Wordsworth is no sentimental liking for country over against city (or it is not *merely* such a liking). It is the appeal of an imaginable human condition which is as close as possible to the state of being we have called "mystical." In one of the most controversial passages from the Preface to the "Lyrical Ballads," Wordsworth says:

> The principal object, then, proposed in these Poems was to choose incidents and situations from common life, and to relate or describe them, throughout, as far as was possible in a selection of language really used by men, and, at the same time, to throw over them a certain colouring of imagination, whereby ordinary things should be presented to the mind in an unusual aspect; and, further, and above all, to make these incidents and situations interesting by tracing in them, truly though not ostentatiously, the primary laws of our nature; chiefly, as regards the manner in which we associate ideas in a state of excitement. Humble and rustic life was generally chosen, because, in that condition, the essential passions of the heart find a better soil in which they can attain their maturity, are less under restraint, and speak a plainer and more emphatic language; because in that condition of life our elementary feelings co-exist in a state of greater simplicity, and consequently, may be more accurately contemplated, and more forcibly communicated; because the manners of rural life germinate from those elementary feelings, and, from the necessary character of rural occupations, are more easily comprehended, and are more durable; and, lastly, because in that condition the passions of men are incorporated with the beautiful and permanent forms of nature.

The language, too, of these men has been adopted (purified indeed from what appear to be its defects, from all lasting and rational causes of dislike or disgust) because such men hourly communicate with the best objects from which the best part of language is originally derived; and because, from their rank in society and the sameness and narrow circle of their intercourse, being less under the influence of social vanity, they convey their feelings and notions in simple and unelaborated expressions. Accordingly, such a language, arising out of repeated experience and regular feelings, is a more permanent, and a far more philosophical language, than that which is frequently substituted for it by Poets, who think that they are conferring honour upon themselves and their art, in proportion as they separate themselves from the sympathies of men, and indulge in arbitrary and capricious habits of expression, in order to furnish food for fickle tastes, and fickle appetites, of their own creation.[17]

The key terms here—"common life," "language really used by men," "ordinary things," "essential passions of the heart," "passions of men," "elementary feelings," and so forth—all suggest more or less the same things, and they all quail before Coleridge's question: what is more common, more real, more essential, more elementary, more ordinary about this language and these situations than any other? [18] The answer is complex. The rural man by whom Wordsworth finds this language "really used" is an ideal image, a fiction, man "ennobled outwardly" before Wordsworth's sight. He is an image of the human personality stripped not only of its "social vanity" and of the artificial and contrived diction which Wordsworth's explanatory Appendix to this Preface claims is what he really means by poetic diction, stripped not only of those social and literary accidents and vices, but also stripped of those cultural, emotional, and even sensory attributes by which we usually identify him. Wordsworth's image of man is of man reduced to certain attributes and passions which Wordsworth regarded as essential, man's capacity for a metaphysical apprehension of the infinite and (that other expression of the same capacity) his hankering after death, unconsciousness, the comatose, the passive, the inert. If it is true that this is his image of essential man, that man is at once ennobled and reduced in Wordsworth's vision of him, then it follows that the language this "man" really uses is going to be a language which is also ennobled and also reduced. That is to say, the language Wordsworth recommends is not a language which can be statistically or sociologically verified by researches among the peasantry of the Lake Country—and could never have been—any more than it will be a language distinguished from the false as rural is distinguished from urban. It will be a language which, in the world's sense, is at least as artificial as any invented by the poets for their exclusive and dandified uses, though in "nature's" sense it will be far more real.

Let us recognize the contradictions at once. Looking at the matter from another side, Wordsworth *did* insist that the language he was proposing was the language of ordinary conversation and that it could be discovered by listening carefully to those involved in "humble and rustic life." He seems to have meant this literally, since otherwise what he says about throwing the color of imagination over such things has no meaning. What happens is that the passage is talking about two things at once, without differentiating between them—as indeed it would have been difficult for Wordsworth to differentiate between them. It is talking about what poetry, the imagination, can do with the raw material of experience, by way of purifying it of its accidents and superficialities, throwing over it a "certain colouring of imagination"; but it is also assuming what Wordsworth would have to assume, that the raw material of the lives of these rural folk is not very raw, that it is already purified, because of their association with the permanent and abiding forms of nature and because of the narrowness and sameness of their occupations and social experience. Wordsworth is always being confused by the differences between his vision of man as ideal and his insistence that this ideal *in fact* exists in such persons as the shepherds of his home country. We have seen how this confusion arises in many different forms in many different poems, and we have talked about how it is probably a necessary confusion, attendant as it is on Wordsworth's metaphysical commitment. Wordsworth says he is going to draw on "incidents and situations from common life"—this means things that could happen to anybody, no extravagant fancies or heroical events. It also means drawn from "humble and rustic life," from the life of a certain class of English society. But it also means drawn from the life which is common to all men, which expresses their common, their shared humanity. His peasants are, in a sense, the lowest common denominator of mankind.

When Dr. Johnson talked about how the state of a man "confined to the employments and pleasures" of the country is "little diversified" and exposed to "few of those accidents which produce perplexities, terrors, and surprises in more complicated transactions," he is saying that the country is fundamentally less *interesting* than the city. Wordsworth uses similar expressions to praise the country, because to him its lack of diversification, of the accidents of human experience, gives it a better chance of being close to the essential experience of mankind. When Wordsworth talks about the language "really used" by men, we cannot understand him unless we understand that he means the language used by men when they are *really* men, when they are in as immediate touch with the eternal as possible. It was his desire to search through experience and language for the kernel of harmony and divinity at their centers. The theory outlined in the Preface is reductive: it is the delineation of a poetic subject reduced to the essentials of experience. And the essentials of experience are not what Dr. Johnson, say, would call them, but the experience of relation to the eternal over against the temporal.

We find the heroes of this pastoral attitude in many different guises—in Michael; in the old man of *Animal Tranquillity and Decay*, worn down to the degree that he has nothing left *but* peace; in the *Old Cumberland Beggar*, moving like a holy object through the world; in the ideal shepherds of *The Prelude*; and of course in the great Leech-gatherer. The most extravagant, and in some ways the most illuminating, example of what this reductiveness can mean is the Idiot Boy,[19] the chief character in a poem by which Wordsworth set great store and which he vigorously defended (against the seventeen-year-old John Wilson) by saying:

I have often applied to idiots, in my own mind, that sublime expression of Scripture, that *their life is hidden with God*. They are worshipped, probably from a feeling of this sort, in several parts of the East. Among the Alps, where they are numerous, they are considered, I believe, as a blessing to the family to which they belong. I have, indeed, often looked upon the conduct of fathers and mothers of the lower classes of society towards idiots as the great triumph of the human heart. It is there that we see the strength, disinterestedness, and grandeur of love. . . .[20]

Idiots are for two reasons valuable objects of the poet's regard: "their life is hidden with God"; and they are objects of the love of man which show that love in its greatest strength and purest form.

It is easy to find the second of these in the poem. Old Susan Gale is sick, and Betty Foy, the idiot's mother, is caring for her. But when Betty sends her boy to town for a doctor and after a long time he does not return, she leaves her patient to go look for him. She goes to the doctor's house, but the boy has not been there, and in her distraction she forgets all about telling the doctor to go to Susan, and hurries off into the night, searching for her child everywhere. At last she finds him sitting on his pony by a waterfall, and as she rejoices in having found him, Susan Gale, cured as if "by magic," hurries to the scene to share her joy. When they ask the boy what he had been doing all that time, he replies:

> "The cocks did crow to-whoo, to-whoo,
> And the sun did shine so cold!"
> —Thus answered Johnny in his glory,
> And that was all his travel's story.

It is easy to trace the "strength" and "disinterestedness" of the mother's love—the strongest proof of it is that it makes her forget the distress of her old friend. But what about the idiot's life being "hidden with God"?

I think the word "glory" has to be taken seriously here. What does the poem teach, after all? That mother love is stronger even than friendship? Yes, but Susan Gale suffered no ill consequences —she was cured. And she was cured as if by magic. The magic was Johnny's association with the moonlight and owls and waterfall, his blessed mindlessness in nature, which amounts to a kind of nighttime wisdom in which ordinary things are reversed, night is day, the moon the sun. In thinking of Johnny rather than Susan, Betty Foy is paying a deep obligation to the irrational forces in nature, to the life which is "hidden with God," and since nature never did betray the heart that loved her, Susan is cured as the sign of nature's approbation of Betty's choice. The poem is not primarily to be understood as a delineation of the psychological processes of a mother's worries. As such it is inept and dull. It is a psychological poem in another sense—concerned with the metaphysical capabilities of the mind, that region which is behind mere intelligence and indifferent to one's ordinary responsibilities in the practical world. Johnny was sent for the doctor, but instead he spent his time in the moonlight and by the waterfall and listening to the owls, and the poem proves him to have been right. When his mother forgot to send the doctor, she did just what her child had done before her, and nature blessed them both.

The boy's idiocy can best be understood by thinking of him as a person from whom intelligence has been stripped, so that there is between him and the natural world *nothing* but his capacity to discover in it its deep hidden secrets. Nature speaks to him directly because there is nothing in his mind to be gotten out of the way. He can be like nature precisely because he is a human being *manqué*.

One hesitates to push such a reading very far because one hesitates to be ridiculous. But it does demonstrate a recognizable tendency in Wordsworth's poetry. We see it in Wordsworth's remarks about another poem, *The Thorn*, though the poem itself is probably not worth examining. Wordsworth says that while traversing the ridge of Quantock Hill one stormy day, he observed a thorn which he had passed many times in bright and calm weather without noticing. He says:

> I said to myself, 'Cannot I by some invention do as much to make this Thorn permanently an impressive object as the storm has made it to my eyes at this moment?' I began the poem accordingly, and composed it with great rapidity.[21]

His further purpose in writing it was to present the thorn as seen through a specially defined pair of eyes, the eyes of a retired mariner who by his idleness has become prone to superstition. He goes on to describe his reasons for choosing such a character:

On which account it appeared to me proper to select a character like this to exhibit some of the general laws by which superstition acts upon the mind. Superstitious men are almost always men of slow faculties and deep feelings; their minds are not loose, but adhesive; they have a reasonable share of imagination, by which word I mean the faculty which produces impressive effects out of simple elements; but they are utterly destitute of fancy, the power by which pleasure and surprise are excited by sudden varieties of situation and an accumulated imagery.

This goes a long way toward explaining the nature of Wordsworth's more grotesque experiments, and it suggests a much more radical and surprising distinction between fancy and imagination than those suggested, for example, by the Preface to the edition of 1815 or even by *The Prelude*.[22] At least it puts the distinctions there set out in a far cruder but therefore somewhat plainer form, and enables us to understand more clearly how a poet so sophisticated, so learned in the traditions of poetry, so deeply cognizant of the proprieties, could so often astonish us by what looks like incredible naïveté or tactlessness in his verse.

We cannot be sure how far the distinction is meant to go. Wordsworth may merely be arguing that on this occasion, in the instance of this one poem, he thought it might be interesting to employ a character who has a share of imagination without having a share of fancy. But one could argue that there is a very characteristic distinction being drawn here, and that Wordsworth is indeed saying that the faculties of imagination and fancy are naturally opposed, since the latter has to do with varieties of situation and an accumulation of imagery, and the former with making simple objects impressive. For the process of making them impressive seems to be a process of resisting variety and of concentrating on the essentials of objects by stripping them of their accidental adornments. Fancy, then, is that which has to do with variety or change; imagination, that which has to do with permanence, sameness, lack of change, and ultimately, as the Preface to 1815 makes clear, the eternal.[23]

But imagination, in this case, is something with which a man of "slow faculties" as well as "deep feelings" is endowed, and one possible implication of this is that deep feelings are somehow a consequence of slow faculties, and furthermore that "imagination" is another word for both these qualities. This poses the imagination as the enemy of wit, even of intelligence if intelligence is an interested response to a variety of situations and if it occasions an accumulation of imagery. Behind the witty and interested intelligence is that region of the mind which is the counterpart of and response to the permanent and abiding forms in nature. In front of those forms are the obtrusive images of the temporal scene, in which the intelligence interests itself. Both intelligence and the temporal scene must be obliterated, or their obtrusiveness ameliorated, before the metaphysical contact can be made. It is even not too much to say that the metaphysical capacity of the mind is a kind of stupidity, being "in a stupor" as far as one's ordinary interests are concerned.

Again, we are dealing with a *tendency* in Wordsworth and not always a very sharply defined one. One day Wordsworth saw a tree and saw it during a storm, when clearness of vision could not distract him from concentrating on it. He cast about to find a way to reproduce this experience in poetry, and found a narrator who was a man of slow faculties and without much share of fancy—a man, in short, whose slow-wittedness was the equivalent of dim weather, so that he could obstinately concentrate on the deep meaning of things rather than on their various and interesting accidents.

His state of mind is like the twilight described in one of the sonnets:

> Hail, Twilight, sovereign of one peaceful hour!
> Not dull art thou as undiscerning Night;
> But studious only to remove from sight
> Day's mutable distinctions.—Ancient Power!
> Thus did the waters gleam, the mountains lower,
> To the rude Briton, when, in wolf-skin vest
> Here roving wild, he laid him down to rest
> On the bare rock, or through a leafy bower
> Looked ere his eyes were closed. By him was seen
> The self-same Vision which we now behold,
> At thy meek bidding, shadowy Power! brought forth;
> These mighty barriers, and the gulf between;
> The flood, the stars,—a spectacle as old
> As the beginning of the heavens and earth!

The poem puts it if anything too bluntly and schematically. The twilight is the hour in which one is most passive, in which one does nothing but observe. And one does not observe very clearly then, with an eye for differences and distinctions, but finds in the very indistinctness of outlines the unity one so much desires. And one is reminded of a state of being which in historical terms is what childhood is in biographical or personal terms, the age of "rude Britons," without knowledge or civilization, without any of the superficialities which plague us in our modern, which is to say our human, involvements. The twilight is the reductive and simplifying hour, which enables us to have some surcease from the complexities of things.

A more curious and subtle example, which also will help us define more exactly a problem in tone raised by this version of pastoral, is *The Danish Boy*:

I

Between two sister moorland rills
There is a spot that seems to lie
Sacred to flowerets of the hills,
And sacred to the sky.
And in this smooth and open dell
There is a tempest-stricken tree;
A corner-stone by lightning cut,
The last stone of a lonely hut;
And in this dell you see
A thing no storm can e'er destroy,
The shadow of a Danish Boy.

II

In clouds above, the lark is heard,
But drops not here to earth for rest;
Within this lonesome nook the bird
Did never build her nest.
No beast, no bird, hath here his home;
Bees, wafted on the breezy air,
Pass high above those fragrant bells
To other flowers:—to other dells
Their burdens do they bear;
The Danish Boy walks here alone:
The lovely dell is all his own.

III

A Spirit of noon-day is he;
Yet seems a form of flesh and blood;
Nor piping shepherd he shall be,
Nor herd-boy of the wood.
A regal vest of fur he wears,
In colour like a raven's wing;
It fears not rain, nor wind, nor dew;
But in the storm 'tis fresh and blue
As budding pines in spring;
His helmet has a vernal grace,
Fresh as the bloom upon his face.

IV

A harp is from his shoulder slung;
Resting the harp upon his knee,
To words of a forgotten tongue
He suits its melody.
Of flocks upon the neighbouring hill
He is the darling and the joy;
And often, when no cause appears,
The mountain-ponies prick their ears,
—They hear the Danish Boy,
While in the dell he sings alone
Beside the tree and corner-stone.

V

There sits he; in his face you spy
No trace of a ferocious air,
Nor ever was a cloudless sky
So steady or so fair.
The lovely Danish Boy is blest
And happy in his flowery cove:
From bloody deeds his thoughts are far;
And yet he warbles songs of war,
That seem like songs of love,
For calm and gentle is his mien;
Like a dead Boy he is serene.

The place he lives in seems to be sacred to the flowers and sky.
It is a place that has seen storms, though, for there is a "tempest-

stricken tree," and time has worked changes upon the place, for there is only the last stone of a lonely hut. But the Danish Boy is a figure the storms cannot touch; he is a "thing no storm can e'er destroy, / The shadow of a Danish Boy." According to the ballad these stanzas were orginally intended to introduce, the Boy was the spirit of a Danish prince who had fled from battle and had been murdered by the inhabitant of a cottage where he had taken refuge. The "Spirit of the Youth, it was believed, haunted the Valley where the crime had been committed." These stanzas, however, make nothing of the legend, and it is fair to read the poem as a distinct and complete work of art.

The dell is beautiful, and the spirit of the boy lives in it like the spirit of an eternal spring: his "regal vest of fur" is black, but in the storm " 'tis fresh and blue / As budding pines in spring"; and his helmet "has a vernal grace, / Fresh as the bloom upon his face." There is "no trace of a ferocious air" in his expression: it is as "steady" and as "fair" as a "cloudless sky." As he makes storms seem mild as budding spring, so his songs, though their subject is war, seem like "songs of love." It is as though he were the perpetual principle or presiding spirit over all things pleasant and harmonious in the universe.

But though the lark can be heard singing over this vale, it "drops not here to earth for rest." "No beast, no bird, hath here his home"; the very bees fly high above this valley and carry their burdens to other dells. "The Danish Boy walks here alone: / The lovely dell is all his own." And the last line of the poem is the most puzzling of all. The Danish Boy is praised and admired for the calm and gentleness of his expression, but the poet says: "Like a dead Boy he is serene."

It is mainly a problem in tone—in the relation of the speaker to his material and to us. How are we meant to hear the news that no lark ever built her nest in this valley, and that the bees shun it? The last two lines of stanza two—"The Danish Boy walks here alone: / The lovely dell is all his own"—seem to tell us we are hearing more reasons why we should admire the boy. It is even hard to find irony in "Like a dead Boy he is serene," for the speaker apparently finds nothing at all disturbing about it. For us the material contains the possibility of all sorts of irony; for the speaker it does not. The Danish Boy is somehow the spirit of harmony and of life constantly renewing itself, perpetual spring; but he is himself so removed from that life that he can have nothing to do with the world of living things. The speaker makes no account of this in his tone; the latent ironies are unexplored.

The speaker and his audience are, like all the natural world, on the outside looking in. Coming upon this valley we "see" the "shadow of a Danish Boy," but he is still walking there alone and "the lovely dell is all his own." The speaker's attitude toward all this is quite different from ours—though we may be tempted to find irony in that extraordinary second stanza, he does not. The poem fulfills half of Mr. Empson's formula for pastoral: it is a case of the complex man, who lives among the disharmonies and storms of the outside world, contemplating this figure of simple harmony and grace, the Danish Boy. But the poem never suggests that the speaker is "in one way worse, in another better" than the boy, though there are the most extraordinary opportunities to say so. The boy is always the better. He speaks a language unintelligible to us, but it is a better language than ours, and the measure of its superiority is its unintelligibility. The larks and bees shun him, and this is rather a rebuke to them that are still involved in time than to him who is beyond it.

In the end the poem expresses the same sort of despair we found in the poems about children, for though this hero seems at first to be the mainspring in the vicissitude of things, a principle of harmony and order in what would otherwise seem to be disorder, he is really something more strange; for he is outside things, in a valley from which they are excluded, and though they may from afar wonder at and appreciate his music, it does not give harmony to them after all. It only emphasizes their own disharmony. There is no real relation between his world and the world in which the poet speaks.

v

WE COME NOW to the final stage of our argument. When we examine these figures in Wordsworth's fiction, in his version of reality, we are likely to forget that in their most important implications they have no objective identity at all, and that the poems know this and tell us so by describing them in terms which suggest they belong to a ballad world or a world of myth. And so we are likely to forget also the main problem before us, with which we began: how does the "love of nature" lead to the "love of man"? For in the end we discover that the speaker in the poems, this poet who claims to have grown to the love of man, is almost always still a lonely man, contemplating in singleness, or at least at a distance from society, the world of nature. Can the formula then be reduced to say: the love of nature leads to the love of nature? And if it can, is it then entirely redundant? If not, in what sense is it not?

Most of the answers are obvious by now. There are two sorts of nature in Wordsworth, temporal and eternal, and the first is in part the medium by which the second expresses itself, though it is also that which hides the eternal from us. Just so, there are two sorts of mind, that which responds to the temporal and that which responds to the eternal, and the first is in part the servant of the second, since only by its interest in the temporal attractions of this world can the demands of the other hope to be satisfied.

In this sense, what we love in man is what is capable of the sacramental act, the temporal part of the mind being fully engaged with the temporal part of nature, so that the metaphysical capacity of the mind and the eternal nature will have avenues by which to make contact with one another. The hero of this act, the man this love of nature leads us to love, is best exemplified by the poet.

But there are other heroes, and other attitudes toward nature, which do not permit such a simple solution. Wordsworth's remembrance of a time when there was no need of the temporal aspect of the mind nor of the temporal nature—or the ideal fiction by which he supposes such a time—engenders in him, in many different poems, where it is expressed in many different ways, a yearning for a more strange and unwordly solution: the mystical contact, immediate and unobstructed, of the metaphysical capabilities of the mind and the eternal presences of nature. More than contact, *identification*. In the world's sense, this identification amounts to death; in eternity's sense, it amounts to life.

The one view accepts temporal nature, and thus accepts (to a degree) the ordinary complexities of our limited human experience, because in accepting them it accepts also the only medium by which contact with eternity can be established. The other view, the mystical yearning, rejects temporal nature, or would do so if it could, because it can be satisfied only by an identification with eternity.

In either case, the formula that the love of nature leads to the love of man can be reduced to the formula that the love of nature leads to the love of nature. For in both cases, the "man" of whom the poems speak is that aspect of his mind which, in one way or another, experiences eternal nature. If we look at it from the sacramental point of view, the metaphysical capacity experiences eternity symbolically, by means of the symbols which nature provides; if we look at it mystically, it experiences eternity immediately and by the rejection of the natural scene—or would do so if it could.

In both cases, the interest of these poems is not primarily in problems of human society or human love, but rather in the relation of each mind—or of the "mind of man" considered abstractly—to the eternal reality of things. It is as if each man stood alone on a promontory, looking away from his fellow men and totally absorbed in the problem of his self and its relation to the abiding, either in itself or as it expresses itself through the temporal scene. This is the egotistical sublime. The love of man is the love of nature because the man whom man loves is himself; or rather, it is that metaphysical capability which he shares with other men and which, in Wordsworth's view, gives them their common significance. And that metaphysical capability can be defined only by its responses to nature, either in the double sense of the sacramental view or in the simple but mysterious mystical view. To love nature properly, in either way, is to love what it makes man capable of, and that love is the love of man.

Still we are the "ordinary reader" who stubbornly insists that this is not enough, or that it is queer and alien. We are accustomed, we insist, to find our significance largely in our relations with our fellow human beings and in realizing that they are different from ourselves, that the accidents or peculiarities of individual personality count for something. The world of Wordsworth finally begins to look like a world of uncluttered lines and proportions —the harmony and relations of things—in which men with no

faces stand back to back and at a distance from one another, gazing at the significance of those lines and proportions.

In *Tintern Abbey* [24] we discover the poet, sitting—apparently
alone—on the banks of the river Wye. At first the scene he contemplates seems full of sensuous particularity, the pleasures of eye
and ear. But soon we discover that the fields and orchards which
might have seemed so individual and particular at first have been
transformed, by a lucky accident of the season, into an indis-
tinguishable unity, and the signs of human habitation too have
been reduced to that unity:

> These plots of cottage-ground, these orchard-tufts,
> Which at this season, with their unripe fruits,
> Are clad in one green hue, and lose themselves
> 'Mid groves and copses. Once again I see
> These hedge-rows, hardly hedge-rows, little lines
> Of sportive wood run wild: these pastoral farms,
> Green to the very door; and wreaths of smoke
> Sent up, in silence, from among the trees!
> With some uncertain notice, as might seem
> Of vagrant dwellers in the houseless woods,
> Or of some Hermit's cave, where by his fire
> The Hermit sits alone.

Certain words begin to ring on our ear: "wild," "secluded," "deep
seclusion." To be wild is to be alien to the human scene, the city,
from which he has come; to be secluded is to be protected from
the pressures of that city, to be alone and far from such involvements.

He says he remembered such a scene during the long five years
he had spent away from it, "in lonely rooms, and 'mid the din /
Of towns and cities," and that he owes to this remembrance of
them "sensations sweet" which have gone so deep as to have become almost visceral or instinctual, "felt in the blood, and felt
along the heart"; and more than that, to have found their way
into the soul, the "purer mind," where they have effected "tranquil restoration." The scene has given him other feelings too,
though these are hard to define, feelings of "unremembered pleasure," of unremembered acts of "kindness and of love." And it has

given him still another gift, "of aspect more sublime," the mood in which "the burthen of the mystery, / In which the heavy and the weary weight / Of all this unintelligible world, / Is lightened." This is the mood in which the paradox of life and death expresses itself, in which "the breath of this corporeal frame / And even the motion of our human blood" are "almost suspended" and we are "laid asleep in body" as the indispensable condition of becoming a "living soul." And in this condition, hardly to be distinguished from physical death, with our eye "made quiet by the power / Of harmony" and by "the deep power of joy," we see into the "life of things."

He has returned to the Wye after an absence of five years, and now "the picture of the mind revives again," and the scene promises once again to give him sustenance with which to bear the trials of future times. He stands looking at the river and thinking about what he was like when he had been there before:

> And so I dare to hope,
> Though changed, no doubt, from what I was when first
> I came among these hills; when like a roe
> I bounded o'er the mountains, by the sides
> Of the deep rivers, and the lonely streams,
> Wherever nature led: more like a man
> Flying from something that he dreads than one
> Who sought the thing he loved. For nature then
> (The coarser pleasures of my boyish days,
> And their glad animal movements all gone by)
> To me was all in all.—I cannot paint
> What then I was. The sounding cataract
> Haunted me like a passion: the tall rock,
> The mountain, and the deep and gloomy wood,
> Their colours and their forms, were then to me
> An appetite; a feeling and a love,
> That had no need of a remoter charm,
> By thought supplied, nor any interest
> Unborrowed from the eye.

This seems at first a celebration of a mere, of a pure and simple, sensuous experience of nature, as if he had not yet discovered his own humanity. And the experience of nature in that way was like the haunting of a passion, was "aching joys" and "dizzy raptures," the satisfying of a deep and simple appetite. Nature then to him was "all in all"—but *which* nature? Was it not both, was this not a time when he did not have to see the distinction between temporal and eternal, so that the mere sensuous experience was the "mystical" also? It is hard to read, for indeed the poem is in some ways vague and it hints at a more precise notion of human development than it really articulates.

Now he stands, grown knowledgeable in the ways of the human world, and he insists that for what he has lost of that time he has received "abundant recompense," two gifts, or perhaps one gift looked at two ways:

> For I have learned
> To look on nature, not as in the hour
> Of thoughtless youth; but hearing oftentimes
> The still, sad music of humanity,
> Nor harsh nor grating, though of ample power
> To chasten and subdue. And I have felt
> A presence that disturbs me with the joy
> Of elevated thoughts; a sense sublime
> Of something far more deeply interfused,
> Whose dwelling is the light of setting suns,
> And the round ocean and the living air,
> And the blue sky, and in the mind of man:
> A motion and a spirit, that impels
> All thinking things, all objects of all thought,
> And rolls through all things. Therefore am I still
> A lover of the meadows and the woods,
> And mountains; and of all that we behold
> From this green earth; of all the mighty world
> Of eye, and ear,—both what they half create,
> And what perceive; well pleased to recognise
> In nature and the language of the sense
> The anchor of my purest thoughts, the nurse,
> The guide, the guardian of my heart, and soul
> Of all my moral being.

He has received the gift of sacramental vision, with its accompanying sense of his own humanity; so that, though he must now view nature more deliberately than before, and under a greater sense of the pressure of having known the city, he knows now what he sees in the landscape—that it is the eternity which in youth he could even ignore because it was so surely there. He has thus, he declares, moved from one kind of joy to another, from a wild joy to a sober one, and the poem is a celebration of that development. He has developed from a love of nature to a love of man, and it has amounted to a different sort of love of nature. He has not, be it noticed, developed a love for *men*, for other human beings, but rather for the "mind of man," for himself or for the mind of man considered abstractly. The poem is never in any doubt about its contempt and fear of the society of mankind, the "dreary intercourse of daily life," the "fretful stir / Unprofitable, and the fever of the world," the "unintelligible world."

The only other human being in the poem, and one for whom he really does appear to feel love, is the "dear, dear Sister" whom he addresses so tenderly. But she is no more than a version of himself at an earlier stage, and the beautiful melancholy which enters the poem when he speaks to her is his nostalgia for that earlier "thoughtless" stage of his life, before the awareness of his own humanity had made the sacramental imagination incumbent on him. He says:

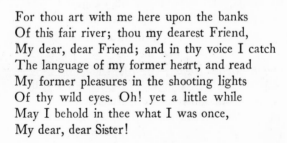

> For thou art with me here upon the banks
> Of this fair river; thou my dearest Friend,
> My dear, dear Friend; and in thy voice I catch
> The language of my former heart, and read
> My former pleasures in the shooting lights
> Of thy wild eyes. Oh! yet a little while
> May I behold in thee what I was once,
> My dear, dear Sister!

And he makes a prayer that she may learn what he has learned, "knowing that Nature never did betray / The heart that loved her," so that her present pleasures may be matured into a "sober pleasure" when her mind "shall be a mansion for all lovely forms," her "memory be as a dwelling-place / For all sweet sounds and harmonies." But his melancholy is a way of saying that in *one* sense, anyway, nature does betray the heart that loves her, that she leaves us vulnerable and distressed in the world of humanity.

It is hard not to sound captious about the poem, and hard not to mistake for a confusion of feeling what may be a complexity of feeling, a contemplated and contained ambivalence. Certainly the poem is moving, and powerfully so, as a contemplation of the deep sources of feeling that we find in our sensuous experience, and of the control of feeling that we gradually learn by distinguishing between ourselves and nature. But it is most moving in what it cannot quite successfully contain, nor contemplate with perfect equanimity: although he says to his sister that her wild participation in nature will so inform her with tranquillity that the evils of men and the dreary intercourse of daily life can never prevail against her nor disturb her cheerful faith, he is the living proof that this is not true. He has returned to the Wye to seclude himself from that world, to participate again as much as possible in its wildness, for what he has learned is not only that love of man which is another form of the love of nature, but a corresponding hatred and fear of the ordinary experience of men.

The ground has been sufficiently prepared to allow us to go on now to a consideration of the great poem which is a summary example of all this. *The Prelude* is the compendium of Wordsworth's attitudes during this period, and it will complete and body forth what we have been able to say so far.

CHAPTER FOUR

The Prelude

The Prelude seems to me to be one of the very great poems in the English language, Wordsworth's supreme achievement. That it has defects, and serious ones, will I think be apparent in our reading of it; but I hope it will also be apparent that these defects are absolutely inseparable from the poem's great virtues, that the defects are as characteristic of the poet's vision as the virtues are, and not mere accidents or lapses. *The Prelude* is the account first of an ideal childhood in nature, then of an adventure into the world of adult and social experience which can also be described as an exile, and finally of a return to that nature which the poet understood as the source and refreshment of whatever strength he had. As we follow the main course of that childhood, that adventure and exile, and that return, I hope it will be possible to give a sense of the marvelous pace, the dazzling versification, above all the strength and sincerity of metaphor and tone without which our assertion that there is also much unresolved ambiguity, even much confusion, will seem captious or niggling. It is often possible, in the criticism of a classical poet like Pope, to assign his defects to fallings away from his characteristic strengths, or to find that he has been diverted into interests which are not central to his vision. But I think our examination of the *Ode* and of *Tintern Abbey* demonstrates adequately that Wordsworth's defects are as central as his virtues. I would even assert that his defects participate essentially in the whole force of the attitudes which produce also the things we find so beautiful in him. To demand that the most important defects and confusions be expunged would in this case be to demand that the poem not be written at all.

I

THE FIRST TWO BOOKS of *The Prelude* are a series of images of man's involvement in mortal nature, and also of the dim and vague revelations he is granted of some other kind of nature. If the ideal childhood is troubled by hints of human corruption, it is also given signs of its possible salvation.

Here is a characteristic passage from the first book:

> Was it for this
> That one, the fairest of all rivers, loved
> To blend his murmurs with my nurse's song,
> And, from his alder shades and rocky falls,
> And from his fords and shallows, sent a voice
> That flowed along my dreams? For this, didst thou,
> O Derwent! winding among grassy holms
> Where I was looking on, a babe in arms,
> Make ceaseless music that composed my thoughts
> To more than infant softness, giving me
> Amid the fretful dwellings of mankind
> A foretaste, a dim earnest, of the calm
> That Nature breathes among the hills and groves.
> When he had left the mountains and received
> On his smooth breast the shadow of those towers
> That yet survive, a shattered monument
> Of feudal sway, the bright blue river passed
> Along the margin of our terrace walk;
> A tempting playmate whom we dearly loved.
> Oh, many a time have I, a five years' child,
> In a small mill-race severed from his stream,
> Made one long bathing of a summer's day;
> Bask'd in the sun, and plung'd and bask'd again
> Alternate, all a summer's day, or scoured
> The sandy fields, leaping through flowery groves
> Of yellow ragwort; or when rock and hill,
> The woods, and distant Skiddaw's lofty height,
> Were bronzed with deepest radiance, stood alone
> Beneath the sky, as if I had been born
> On Indian plains, and from my mother's hut
> Had run abroad in wantonness, to sport
> A naked savage, in the thunder shower.
>
> (ll. 269–300.)

The passage is orchestrated with a sense of the seasons' changes, the changes in weather, the child's involvement in the processes of time; the river itself is an image not only of the flow of the child's own experience, but of the toll historical time takes on man's achievements: the river mirrors the "shadow of those towers / That yet survive, a shattered monument / Of feudal sway." (At the same time, the towers, having survived their own epoch, are an image of man's stubborn resistance to time.) But in this river there is also a music that *composes* his thoughts and gives him "amid the fretful dwellings of mankind" a knowledge of the "calm" that "Nature" can bestow upon the mortal natural scene. "Nature" here is not the same thing as the "hills and groves," but rather something that breathes "calm" among them; and yet it is not to be easily separated from them either. Just so, the river speaks an extraordinary music to the child, but it is the river's music nevertheless; the child's experience of the river hints of some order beyond the ordinary natural scene, yet so intermingled with it as hardly to be distinguished from it. It is an order, a composition, that seems to be in the river itself, that seems indeed to be the very music of the river, and at the same time a composition of the consciousness of the child. It "flowed along his dreams" and was a "foretaste," a "dim earnest" of things he would understand more plainly and clearly when he grew older. The child is not only a creature like any other, involved in change and flux as surely as the river is; he is also the favored pupil of a nature beyond nature.

It was never very clear to him what this informing and eternal nature might be, and its revelations often came to him ambiguously, at moments when he was most aware of his limitations in time:

> Nor less when spring had warmed the cultured Vale,
> Moved we as plunderers where the mother-bird
> Had in high places built her lodge: though mean
> Our object and inglorious, yet the end
> Was not ignoble. Oh! when I have hung
> Above the raven's nest, by knots of grass
> And half-inch fissures in the slippery rock
> But ill-sustained, and almost (so it seemed)
> Suspended by the blast that blew amain,

Shouldering the naked crag, oh, at that time
While on the perilous ridge I hung alone,
With what strange utterance did the loud dry wind
Blow through my ear! the sky seemed not a sky
Of earth—and with what motion moved the clouds!

(ll. 326–339.)

The image of his precarious position on the crag, and the violence
of the loud dry wind about him, represent his precarious and
dangerous position in nature. He is the honored pupil of an immortal nature, privileged to witness one of those transformations
by which the wind becomes a wind not of earth, the clouds'
motion something more than what appears to the mere physical
eye. But he is still clinging to the cliff and still a plunderer of
natural things, and so is both an active and a passive participant in
the processes by which nothing can remain the same, nothing in-
vulnerable to loss and change. It is really impossible to tell
whether the wind blows about him to threaten his life, suspended
there on the crag, or to protest his plundering, or to reveal in its
music the eternal realities of which by virtue of his imagination
he will later become fully conscious. It is all three at once, for it
is the nature of man to be at once in danger of destruction, to be a
destroyer of things, and to be a witness of the indestructible.

When he went among the hills at night, to collect birds from
his (and others') traps, he seemed to be "a trouble to the peace
that dwelt" among the moon and stars shining over him, and on
his way home he heard "among the solitary hills, / Low breath-
ings" coming after him (ll. 315–325); and when he rowed upon
the lake, in someone else's boat, a hill rose up behind him and
strode after him "like a living thing," frightening him so that
he left the lake and took himself home (ll. 357–390). It is true
that in these instances he was doing something wrong and was being rebuked for it by the presences in nature. But the tone of the
passage is certainly deeper than that, its content more puzzling:
these things were more than his scoutmasters, and their hostility
and dangerousness—which yet seemed in some way benevolent—
had to do with more than his childish pranks. It is true, and important, that nature bore a moral or ethical relation to him, but
we would do the passages a disservice to read them only in that

way. He was a trouble to the moon and stars not only because he was doing something wrong, but also simply because he was a human being; for a human being, as a creature of time, is by definition a stranger to the "unknown modes of being" which at the same time he is uniquely equipped to apprehend, and of which moon and stars are the outward expression. After the boy had seen the hill rise up behind him, his brain worked for many days

> with a dim and undetermined sense
> Of unknown modes of being; o'er my thoughts
> There hung a darkness, call it solitude
> Or blank desertion. No familiar shapes
> Remained, no pleasant images of trees,
> Of sea or sky, no colours of green fields;
> But huge and mighty forms, that do not live
> Like living men, moved slowly through the mind
> By day, and were a trouble to my dreams.
>
> (ll. 392–400.)

This is the most explicit instance so far. The revelations of those forms required the removal or obliteration of his ordinary sensuous experience of trees and fields, and perhaps it required also some suspension of rationality or conscious thinking. What these "modes of being" are is at this point very mysterious. One cannot answer, Wordsworth could not answer, certain questions about them. Are they metaphysical presences, beings outside or behind the ordinary nature he knows? Or are they modes of psychological being in himself, new avenues of awareness he has never yet explored, different in kind from his ordinary means of awareness? When he says they "do not live like living men," does he mean they are as utterly unlike men as possible, or does he mean they are like men in every respect but mortality? And why are they so dour and threatening, why is it "pleasant" images that have to be removed? These "huge and mighty forms" are frightening, even sinister, and a "trouble" to his dreams; yet they are extraordinary experiences of the same order as his apprehension of the "calm" Nature which breathes among the hills and groves, or the music in the river.

This instance is ambiguous in the way his experience while

skating is ambiguous. In that rapturous time he skated away from his friends and gave his body to the winds and, spinning round and round, suddenly stopped short:

> yet still the solitary cliffs
> Wheeled by me—even as if the earth had rolled
> With visible motion her diurnal round!
> Behind me did they stretch in solemn train,
> Feebler and feebler, and I stood and watched
> Till all was tranquil as a dreamless sleep.
>
> (ll. 425–463.)

It is easy enough to fix the physiological causes of this vision of things. Yet clearly it is meant to show a special moment of insight. And is that moment, when it seemed he could see the very motion of the earth, a perception into the dimension of time, the very action of time itself; or is it something else, an insight into the eternal, a dimension of "time" other than the one we know? It is both, time and the eternal at their point of conjunction.

Almost every passage in these first two books of the poem, descriptive of his childhood, is saturated and suffused with the same complexity of observations and attitudes. He is always aware of the pressures of time upon him, the "faces of the moving year" (l. 561), the frost raging "bitterly, with keen and silent tooth" outside his doors (l. 537), the year spinning about him with "giddy motion" (Bk. II, ll. 47–48); but he is also aware that there is some shaping toward permanency going on in this very process of time, or that behind the pleasant images of trees there are mighty forms unconditioned by change. And these two sorts of perception are always mingled and entangled with each other. At the age of ten he stood upon the shores of Westmoreland, while his eye moved "o'er many a league of shining water, gathering as it seemed / Through every hair-breadth in that field of light / New pleasures like a bee among the flowers" (Bk. I, ll. 567–580). This was an experience of quietness and peace not unlike the music of Derwent river, and it occurred just at the moment when he was more than usually aware of the process of time, just at the turning of the day into night, when twilight became moonrise, when "the Sea threw off his evening shade, / And to the shepherd's hut on distant hills / Sent welcome notice of the rising moon." He went horseback riding with some of his young friends one day, and rode out to visit a ruined abbey:

> Along the smooth green turf
> Our horses grazed. To more than inland peace
> Left by the west wind sweeping overhead
> From a tumultuous ocean, trees and towers
> In that sequestered valley may be seen,
> Both silent and both motionless alike;
> Such the deep shelter that is there, and such
> The safeguard for repose and quietness.
>
> Our steeds remounted and the summons given,
> With whip and spur we through the chauntry flew
> In uncouth race, and left the cross-legged knight,
> And the stone-abbot, and that single wren
> Which one day sang so sweetly in the nave
> Of the old church, that—though from recent showers
> The earth was comfortless, and touched by faint
> Internal breezes, sobbings of the place
> And respirations, from the roofless walls
> The shuddering ivy dripped large drops—yet still
> So sweetly 'mid the gloom the invisible bird
> Sang to herself, that there I could have made
> My dwelling-place, and lived forever there
> To hear such music. Through the walls we flew
> And down the valley, and, a circuit made
> In wantonness of heart, through rough and smooth
> We scampered homewards. Oh, ye rocks and streams,
> And that still spirit shed from evening air!
> Even in this joyous time I sometimes felt
> Your presence, when with slackened step we breathed
> Along the sides of the steep hills, or when
> Lighted by gleams of moonlight from the sea
> We beat with thundering hoofs the level sand.
>   (Bk. II, ll. 107–137.)

The valley they enter is "sequestered," "silent," "motionless," a "safeguard for repose and quietness." An invisible bird is singing there, so sweetly that he could have stayed there forever to hear its music, and could have made the abbey his dwelling place. But it is not a dwelling place; time has touched it already, and the signs of the earth's life—and therefore of its vulnerability to time—are all about him. So he has to leave, the creature of time prevented by his involvement in the life of change from experiencing the timeless. The place of quiet is not an experience of the eternal after all, but an illusion of it. Yet it is an expressive illusion. It defines at once the goal of all his seeking, the quietness and repose of an experience of the eternal, and the way in which time, his ordinary experience of things, prevents him from reaching his goal. The ruined abbey, like the shattered tower mirrored in Derwent, is an image at once of decay and of resistance to decay, and the bird's song, like the music of the river, expresses the composition and continuity that exists in nature behind the changeful appearance of things, and the composition that is being built up in his own mind. But whatever it expresses, the bird is in fact only a bird after all, and its music only an analogue to that mysterious music he wants—and yet is afraid—to hear.

These scenes from the poet's childhood demonstrate, then, a harmony between man and both sorts of nature. He has in his childhood a kind of simple delight in the rivers and hills and woods, and he grows increasingly more conscious of that delight. He has extraordinary experiences of the other sort of nature, which reveals itself to him either in states of profound calm or in majestic and, though frightening, nevertheless thrilling images. But if there is harmony, there is also a tension and even a conflict between him and both sorts of nature; for he plunders the one, and his relations with the other, the eternal, are both sporadic and fleeting. The music he hears he cannot hear forever, though he would like to. His own simple childish joy, his boyhood pleasures, prevent him, and his limitation in time prevents him as well. This part of the poem is never still, never rests in one season or hour; in the same way, his communion with the eternal is always thwarted.

There are a number of passages in these first two books, however, most of them more general and speculative than the ones we have been observing, which celebrate in triumphant and exulting terms a solution to this very problem. This solution is implied in and explicitly derived from the two metaphors of music and of a building, which occur and recur in these books. What the metaphors seem to be saying is this: Wordsworth's early experience of the hills and groves, the rivers and valleys, was the beginning of his education in a certain way of seeing things, the building of a structure in his mind which would be able to contain and express and even *be* certain meanings in and beyond the world. The raw material of these meanings is his experience of the changefulness of his natural environment and his experience of his own passions; but, having been built, having been composed, they are transmuted from their gross impermanence into that which can withstand and defeat change, and the passions are purified and exalted into a kind of religious "delight" or "joy," which is a passion defined by its transcendence over all others. "Dust as we are," says Wordsworth,

> Dust as we are, the immortal spirit grows
> Like harmony in music; there is a dark
> Inscrutable workmanship that reconciles
> Discordant elements, makes them cling together
> In one society. How strange that all
> The terrors, pains, and early miseries,
> Regrets, vexations, lassitudes interfused
> Within my mind, should e'er have borne a part,
> And that a needful part, in making up
> The calm existence that is mine when I
> Am worthy of myself! Praise to the end!
> Thanks to the means which Nature deigned to employ;
> Whether her fearless visitings, or those
> That came with soft alarm, like hurtless light
> Opening the peaceful clouds; or she may use
> Severer interventions, ministry
> More palpable, as best might suit her aim.
>
> (Bk. I, ll. 340–356.)

The ideal state of mind with which to confront the universe—or rather, with which to participate in and be at one with the universe —is a state of "calm," of peacefulness and repose. This calm is the mind's response to its own perception of the "affinities" of things, of the permanent relations whereby the world about us has an identity greater than the sum of its parts. This calm is the harmonizing of one's varied experience of all phenomena, derived from "gloom and tumult" no less than from "fair / And tranquil scenes" (Bk. II, ll. 323–324). So it was that Wordsworth could derive the same feeling of exultation from walking "under the quiet stars" as he could from standing beneath a rock when the night "blackened with a coming storm." Then he heard

> notes that are
> The ghostly language of the ancient earth,
> Or make their dim abodes in distant winds.
> Thence did I drink the visionary power;
> And deem not profitless those fleeting moods
> Of shadowy exultation: not for this,
> That they are kindred to our purer mind
> And intellectual life; but that the soul,
> Remembering how she felt, but what she felt
> Remembering not, retains an obscure sense
> Of possible sublimity, whereto
> With growing faculties she doth aspire,
> With faculties still growing, feeling still
> That whatsoever point they gain, they yet
> Have something to pursue.
>   (Bk. II, ll. 302–322.)

The "Wisdom and Spirit" of the universe built up out of the "forms and images" of the world a "breath / And everlasting motion" and "intertwined" for him "The passions that build up our human soul" (Bk. I, ll. 401–407), and did it without his conscious knowledge; so that whatever he did, however "mean" or "inglorious" his motive, the "end was not ignoble" (ll. 326–330). More and more, as he grew older, he began to realize the nature of what the wisdom of the universe was doing for him, and his interest in nature became more and more conscious as he began actively to desire such experiences of exaltation. By the end of the second book he is able to say triumphantly:

> The song would speak
> Of that interminable building reared
> By observation of affinities
> In objects where no brotherhood exists
> To passive minds. My seventeenth year was come;

And, whether from this habit rooted now
So deeply in my mind, or from excess
In the great social principle of life
Coercing all things into sympathy,
To unorganic natures were transferred
My own enjoyments; or the power of truth
Coming in revelation, did converse
With things that really are; I, at this time,
Saw blessings spread around me like a sea.
Thus while the days flew by, and years passed on,
From Nature and her overflowing soul,
I had received so much, that all my thoughts
Were steeped in feeling; I was only then
Contented, when with bliss ineffable
I felt the sentiment of Being spread
O'er all that moves and all that seemeth still;
O'er all that, lost beyond the reach of thought
And human knowledge, to the human eye
Invisible, yet liveth to the heart;
O'er all that leaps and runs, and shouts and sings,
Or beats the gladsome air; o'er all that glides
Beneath the wave, yea in the wave itself,
And mighty depth of waters. Wonder not
If high the transport, great the joy I felt,
Communing in this sort through earth and heaven
With every form of creature, as it looked
Towards the Uncreated with a countenance
Of adoration, with an eye of love.
One song they sang, and it was audible,
Most audible, then, when the fleshly ear,
O'ercome by humblest prelude of that strain,
Forgot her functions, and slept undisturbed.

(ll. 382–418.)

The passage is triumphant, and beautifully so, with the dignity of its allusions to Genesis and with its sustained tone of religious joy. It is a powerful statement of faith in the "sentiment of Being" which can put together what has been asunder and make music of what has been merely disparate. It is very beautiful, but there is room to wonder whether it does not, however grandly, ignore some of the tensions between the changeful and the unchanging that we have seen so powerfully expressed in other passages. Indeed, there is room to consider whether most of the passages of generalization, in these first two books, do not oversimplify the problems his experience had presented to him. Man, for Wordsworth, is involved in and conditioned by time; he is the victim of his own hours and seasons. But he has saving links to that quietness and peace which lie outside time and yet inform it. This is a notion very difficult to comprehend and very liable to oversimplification. Wordsworth claims that the human being can and does grow through experience into a consciousness of those saving links which defeat time. But the notions of growth and experience are *themselves* notions of time! One of the most famous passages in the poem is an example of the oversimplification which can result when this problem is scanted or ignored:

> Blest the infant Babe,
> (For with my best conjecture I would trace
> Our Being's earthly progress,) blest the Babe,
> Nursed in his Mother's arms, who sinks to sleep
> Rocked on his Mother's breast; who with his soul
> Drinks in the feelings of his Mother's eye!
> For him, in one dear Presence, there exists
> A virtue which irradiates and exalts
> Objects through widest intercourse of sense.
> No outcast he, bewildered and depressed:
> Along his infant veins are interfused
> The gravitation and the filial bond
> Of nature that connect him with the world.
> Is there a flower, to which he points with hand
> Too weak to gather it, already love
> Drawn from love's purest earthly fount for him
> Hath beautified that flower; already shades
> Of pity cast from inward tenderness
> Do fall around him upon aught that bears
> Unsightly marks of violence and harm.
> Emphatically such a Being lives
> Frail creature as he is, helpless as frail,
> An inmate of this active universe.
> For feeling has to him imparted power
> That through the growing faculties of sense
> Doth like an agent of the one great Mind
> Create, creator and receiver both,
> Working but in alliance with the works
> Which it beholds.   (Bk. II, ll. 232–260.)

Such a passage makes the whole relationship of man and nature seem much less difficult than it is. The mother is the agent or fountain of love in the world. From her the child imbibes its capacities for love, and its love is expressed by all its sensuous relationships with the world around it. All this love of earthly things works hand in hand with the "one great Mind" of the universe. The "growing faculties of sense" suggest that the infant will grow into more and more intimate relations with the "one great Mind," and will do so inevitably, out of the exigencies of its own being.

This beautiful passage is misleading in three ways: first, it suggests an oversimple analogy between the love of humanity and the love of natural objects—is the child to the flower necessarily what the mother is to the child?; second, it suggests that our "Being" has an "earthly *progress*" which is perfectly natural and *inevitably* fortunate; third, it suggests that the vehicle of this progress is in some perfectly easy way the growing powers of the senses. These things are stated as though universally true and applicable to all men, but really they are a statement of faith, a vision of what *ought* to be. Wordsworth was never able to make up his mind between such an optimistic view of men's state and another view which says that the ordinary man, involved in growth and decay, is progressively estranged by his experience of the world from that "great Mind," and that even the poet, who is specially fortunate in his capacities for communion with the infinite, must undergo an exile or estrangement, and can achieve this communion only by learning how to defeat experience. *The Ode: Intimations of Immortality* is a case in point.

Indeed, signs of the stress and strain between these views are apparent even in this passage. It talks about the "growing faculties of sense," but it also looks back nostalgically toward the infant state as one especially, even mysteriously, blessed; and it recognizes that the natural world the child looks out on is marred by "unsightly marks of violence or harm." But it does not recognize the degree to which these considerations might modify and even contradict its explicit doctrine. The passage is a celebration of

> that calm delight
> Which, if I err not, surely must belong
> To those first-born affinities that fit
> Our new existence to existing things,

And, in our dawn of being, constitute
The bond of union between life and joy.
(Bk. I, ll. 553–558.)

But it does not recognize what other passages in the poem do recognize—that in the very nature of man and in the mortal natural scene which is his environment there are things that obstruct "affinities" and separate us from the "one great Mind."

We are considering these things as applying not only to Wordsworth but to all men. The relationship of man to nature is exceedingly complex. If all there was to man was only his metaphysical capability, everything would be as pure and simple as a geometry problem perpetually being solved by an abstract geometrician. If man were wholly conditioned by time—had no such metaphysical capability, was never aware of the huge and mighty forms behind the pleasant images of trees—and if nature were wholly mortal, the anguishing possibility of immortality would never arise. But man and nature exist together in a mutually creative and destructive relationship; they help each other grow, and they help destroy one another. The young boy clinging to the naked crag is at the elements' mercy, while at the same time he is plundering a bird's nest. And the man who wants to get past the mortal scene into the repose of the eternal must get past not only the familiar shapes and pleasant images of perishing trees, but also past the passions and vicissitudes of his own mind. Man is uniquely aware of his involvement in change and death. He observes himself growing up and growing old; he is self-conscious. And to be self-conscious, to carry his consciousness of change and coming death about with him, is to be like a destroyer in nature. It is necessary to see the withering in the new flower, the spavining in the colt. To see it is almost as if to cause it. Adam ate of the fruit of the Tree of Knowledge and knew there was death. He was therefore henceforth an intruder in the Garden and, as it were, its destroyer.

I I

IN THE FIRST two books of *The Prelude*, Wordsworth frequently mentions the other boys who had gone with him on his rambles, had skated or gone horseback riding with him; but these figures are shadowy, almost projections of himself, and have no distinct meaning in themselves. The third book, however, is something different, for there the young Wordsworth comes in contact with people who had not shared his fortunate environment and whose habits of life are therefore radically different from his own. This is putting it somewhat mildly: at Cambridge the poet was introduced to the great world of men, and found that world alien to his own spirit.

The book is complicated by the collision between the poet's powerful and honest sense of fact and his thematic preconceptions. (Indeed, this is true of the whole poem, and is one way of stating my main point about it.) We are given wonderfully vivid impressions of what Cambridge must have looked like—the sounds from its kitchens, the bustle of its crowds at morning convocations, the idle pastimes of its students. We are told that the poet got little from the conventional curriculum, and this statement is accompanied by a handsome admission that he brought to the curriculum a mind ill suited for it. If this were all, we might be justified in reading the book as an especially painstaking and careful piece of naturalistic autobiography. But when all is said and done, our dominant feeling about it has to be, not that it is a piece of scrupulous biographical reporting, but that Cambridge was a metaphor for him, that it had a thematic meaning which was to be repeated and repeated in all his exchanges with society wherever he went.

It will not be clear at once—not until after we have examined some passages—how these things collide, or why there should be any real opposition between them.

Cambridge was a whirlpool that "seemed to suck us in with an eddy's force" (l. 14); it was a magic transformation or enchantment of himself, as if "the change / Had waited on some Fairy's wand" (ll. 35–36); a "dazzling" (l. 90) or a "novel" "show" (l. 205); a tournament, a fair or carnival (l. 586); a change of clothes, as in the theater ("Such was the tenor of the second act / In this new life") (ll. 259–260); a siesta or "noon-tide rest" (l. 334); an attractive but unsound floating island in the sea (ll. 335–339); a "deep vacation" (l. 512). These metaphors tell their own story. Cambridge was an experience of unreality, of the irresponsibility of a holiday; it was attractive with the specious attractiveness of magic. It had all the dangers of bewilderment and distraction, and for a time the poet appeared to be lost among its illusive charms:

> Not seeking those who might participate
> My deeper pleasures (nay, I had not once,
> Though not unused to mutter lonesome songs,
> Even with myself divided such delight,
> Or looked that way for aught that might be clothed
> In human language), easily I passed
> From the remembrance of better things,
> And slipped into the ordinary works
> Of careless youth, unburthened, unalarmed.
> *Caverns* there were within my mind which sun
> Could never penetrate, yet did there not
> Want store of leafy *arbours* where the light
> Might enter in at will. Companionships,
> Friendships, acquaintances, were welcome all.
> We sauntered, played, or rioted; we talked
> Unprofitable talk at morning hours;
> Drifted about along the streets and walks,
> Read lazily in trivial books, went forth
> To gallop through the country in blind zeal
> Of senseless horsemanship, or on the breast
> Of Cam sailed boisterously, and let the stars
> Come forth, perhaps without one quiet thought.
>
> (ll. 237–258.)

His time was spent mostly among the frivolous and idle, his eyes were "crossed by butterflies, ears vexed / By chattering popinjays" (ll. 446–447). Everywhere he looked he saw the

> scenes as obsolete in freaks
> Of character, in points of wit as broad,
> As aught by wooden images performed
> For entertainment of the gaping crowd
> At wake or fair.
>
> (ll. 570–576.)

The reader protests a little at such metaphors and similes, and at the tone with which this freshman life is described. Will a mere undergraduate laziness, for example, bear all the solemn weight of "blind zeal" of "senseless horsemanship" (ll. 254–256), and can the reader's sense of humor bear the poet's condemnation of his own "vague / And loose indifference, easy likings, aims / Of a low pitch—duty and zeal dismissed" (ll. 327–329)? We are inclined to murmur that boys will be boys and to put all this down to pompous egotism. But the truth is that Wordsworth is confronted here, as in many later books of the poem, with an insoluble artistic problem, the problem of matching harmoniously his (and our) common-sense view of what his undergraduate experience must have been with the thematic significance he had to give it. Certainly the poet himself makes it plain enough how aware he is that his idleness and vanity in those days were not very serious matters. His days were not given up to "wilful alienation from the right, / Or walks of open scandal" (ll. 325–327), and he was never *entirely* idle. His story is in fact probably the story of most undergraduates, anywhere, at any time. But the important thing is that it meant something different to him.

To him, Cambridge was symbolic or emblematic not of the life an undergraduate is likely to fall into, but of the great world of social experience itself. Cambridge was a scene that expressed in dwarf proportions

> The limbs of the great world; its eager strifes
> Collaterally pourtrayed, as in mock fight,
> A tournament of blows, some hardly dealt
> Though short of mortal combat; and whate'er
> Might in this pageant be supposed to hit
> An artless rustic's notice, this way less,
> More that way, was not wasted upon me—
> And yet the spectacle may well demand
> A more substantial name, no mimic show,
> Itself a living part of a live whole,
> A creek in the vast sea; for, all degrees
> And shapes of spurious fame and short-lived praise
> Here sate in state, and fed with daily alms
> Retainers won away from solid good;
> And here was Labour, his own bond-slave; Hope,
> That never set the pains against the prize;
> Idleness halting with his weary clog,

And poor misguided Shame, and witless Fear,
And simple Pleasure foraging for Death;
Honour misplaced, and Dignity astray;
Feuds, factions, flatteries, enmity, and guile
Murmuring submission, and bald government,
(The idol weak as the idolater,)
And Decency and Custom starving Truth,
And blind Authority beating with his staff
The child that might have led him; Emptiness
Followed as of good omen, and meek Worth
Left to herself unheard of and unknown.

(ll. 583–611.)

And so the solemn metaphors, the solemn tone, are intelligible, for they express not the facts, nor the common-sense view of what Cambridge must have been to a young boy going there for the first time, but something larger, a total view of society itself. What a view it is! It moves from the neutral "limbs of the great world" and "eager strifes" through line after line expressing his hatred and disgust at what he found there. Even supposing Cambridge deserved such a condemnation, the important thing is the connection he makes with the world outside it. This passage is about the world in general, and about Cambridge only as an example of that world, a "creek in the vast sea." It remains to discover the nature and cause of his antipathy to the world.

But there is another important question to raise first. The metaphors, and the explicit account, tell us the experience was bewildering and full of distracting illusions. But there is still some question how nearly these things could touch him, whether he could be harmed by them at all. A charmed island has its dangers, but not for the mariner who is preserved from its charms by a surf that "scared him thence" or by a wind that "blew / Inexorably adverse" (ll. 486–493). A vacation may involve the danger of irresponsibility, but the very notion of a vacation implies its end and a return to the workaday world. A dazzling show, a theatrical entertainment, may be designed to hide the truth of things, but eventually the show is over and the audience goes out again into reality. Wordsworth was tempted into unsuitable company and vain ways, but there were still "caverns" inviolate

in him, and there were still times when he slipped away from
the dazzling press of trivialities and renewed his relationship to

> universal things; perused
> The common countenance of earth and sky:
> Earth, nowhere unembellished by some trace
> Of that first Paradise whence man was driven;
> And sky, whose beauty and bounty are expressed
> By the proud name she bears—the name of Heaven.
>
> (ll. 109–114.)

"Imagination slept, / And yet not utterly" (ll. 260–261). Though
he moved through this life at Cambridge like one bewitched by
its most superficial attractions and temptations, there was still a
power in him which had known better things than the books he
slighted, and which had left "less space within" his mind for even
the most praiseworthy things Cambridge might have offered.
The dangers and temptations he describes were in a sense not dangers and temptations for *him*, since he was protected against them
by his past experience of nature.

This raises still another question. First we have been saying
that Wordsworth took Cambridge too seriously, that he adopted
too solemn a tone in his description of it; then we have been saying
that, in a sense, he did not take it as seriously as most people would,
that he revealed how he was almost untouched by it and absolutely
protected from its influence. We shall see that these observations
are only apparently, and by a trick of words, opposed to each other.
Wordsworth moved through Cambridge like an enchanted warrior,
who could be wounded but whose wounds were always miraculously healed; or he was a warrior who could not be defeated,
for whenever he was in danger, his patron covered him with a
cloud and made him safe from any adversary. So the experience of
battle was not meaningful to him, in the terms by which we usually understand "experience." On the other hand, for such an enchanted and privileged figure, all experience was unusually meaningful in a contemplative or symbolic, though not in a dramatic,
sense. Wordsworth came to Cambridge armed with his memories
of his metaphysical experiences of that eternal nature which lies
behind the natural scene. Perhaps he did not know yet that they

were metaphysical, but metaphysical they were, whether he knew it or not: they were experiences within time of something whose province is independent of time. Ordinary experience, then, the dimension of time, could have little significance except insofar as it gave evidence of the eternal which lay behind it, but insofar as it *could* give such evidence it was extraordinarily meaningful. For in that case, every event, everything the poet perceived in his wanderings, *could* express the eternal. But more of this later. It is only necessary here to have noticed the peculiarities in his vision of Cambridge, the ease with which he generalizes it into an image of the whole social world, and the condemnation of society which—apparently inevitably—ensues.

The poet first entered that great world of which Cambridge had been a sort of preview when he went to London. Once again everything was hubbub and noise, dazzling and confusing, and to be there was as though to be carried, without will, by an irresistible tide. London, like Cambridge, was the place of illusions and distractions, distortion and magic. And, as at Cambridge, though he suffered from these things, they could not really touch him.

He speaks of London as a "monstrous ant-hill on the plain / Of a too-busy world" (Bk. VII, ll. 149–150), and "endless stream of men and moving things" (l. 151), a "string of dazzling wares, / Shop after shop, with symbols, blazened names" (ll. 157–158), where the fronts of houses were like the title pages of huge books (ll. 160–161), and giant posters crowded forward against the eye (ll. 194–195). "All specimens of man" could be seen there, but what he noticed mainly were the exotics, the Indians, Moors, Russians, Chinese, Malays; and the distorted, like the "travelling cripple, by the trunk cut short, / And stumping on his arms" (ll. 189–228).

The whole city was, as Cambridge had been, a kind of theater for him, in both senses—merely an illusion of reality, and merely an entertainment, an interlude in the serious business of his life. He talks about the paintings and sculptures he saw, "those sights that ape / The absolute presence of reality" (ll. 232–235), and he talks about the fascination of pantomimes and the drama, Jack the Giant Killer walking the stage with the word "Invisible" flaming on his chest (ll. 279–287), and Mrs. Siddons holding forth on a stage where all the ages and conditions of man were represented. This was an "enchanting age and sweet! / Romantic, almost," as if he had been led into a "dazzling cavern of romance" (ll. 401–457). He looks back on it with a good deal of pleasure, it is true, but apologetically so, and finds it necessary to assure us that this "storm" of pleasure and enchantment "passed not beyond the suburbs of the mind" (ll. 475–476). It was city against city, London against the city of himself, and though London had its effects, he prevailed. As at Cambridge, the imagination "slept" (l. 469). But, as at Cambridge, it was still finally inviolable.

The trouble with London was not so much that it provided distracting entertainments such as these, but that things "titled higher," the serious pursuits of urban man, were themselves no more than entertainments, theatrical and false. So it is that he describes the lawyers orating in their courts or in Parliament, that "great stage / Where senators, tongue-favored men, perform" (ll. 486–511). With heavy and explicit irony, he describes the orator in action:

> Silence! hush!
> This is no trifler, no short-flighted wit,
> No stammerer of a minute, painfully
> Delivered. No! the Orator hath yoked
> The Hours, like young Aurora, to his car:
> Thrice welcome Presence! how can patience e'er
> Grow weary of attending on a track
> That kindles with such glory! All are charmed,
> Astonished; like a hero in romance,
> He winds away his never-ending horn;
> Words follow words, sense seems to follow sense:
> What memory and what logic! till the strain
> Transcendent, superhuman as it seemed,
> Grows tedious even in a young man's ear.

And he goes on to describe how even the pulpit became a stage, where the shepherd of the flock was not a pastor so much as a shepherd out of some elaborate and effete romance, calling on all learning, both good and bad, to make

ornaments and flowers
To entwine the crook of eloquence that helped
This pretty Shepherd, pride of all the plains,
To rule and guide his captivated flock.

(ll. 543–572.)

It is true that even in this city of singularities and lies he found types and symbols of that elemental grace and virtue he so much admired, but these were as set apart from the hubbub as he himself essentially was:

But foolishness and madness in parade,
Though most at home in this their dear domain,
Are scattered everywhere, no rarities,
Even to the rudest novice of the Schools.
Me, rather, it employed to note, and keep
In memory, those individual sights
Of courage, or integrity, or truth,
Or tenderness, which there, set off by foil,
Appeared more touching. One will I select;
A Father—for he bore that sacred name—
Him saw I, sitting in an open square,
Upon a corner-stone of that low wall,
Wherein were fixed the iron pales that fenced
A spacious grass-plot; there, in silence, sate
This One Man, with a sickly babe outstretched
Upon his knee, whom he had hither brought
For sunshine, and to breathe the fresher air.

(ll. 594–610.)

When he wandered "lost / Amid the moving pageant" and saw the figure of a blind beggar propped against a wall, the tide that had been carrying him through the flux and flow of the city suddenly turned, "as with the might of waters," and it seemed to him that he had been admonished "from another world" (ll. 635–649).

There were also moments in the life of the city itself when it took on a very great beauty, but these were moments when its ordinary activities were quieted as in a sort of grave:

the peace
That comes with night; the deep solemnity
Of nature's intermediate hours of rest,

When the great tide of human life stands still;
The business of the day to come, unborn,
Of that gone by, locked up, as in the grave;
The blended calmness of the heavens and earth,
Moonlight and stars, and empty streets, and sounds
Unfrequent as in deserts . . .

Then even the voice of a whore could become beautiful, when its purport was not listened to. The city was most beautiful when most unlike itself (ll. 650–668).

The poet himself distrusts these experiences of beauty and tranquillity, and turns to what he thinks of as a more accurate image or symbol, "epitome," of what the city is—Bartholomew Fair, a work that lays the whole "creative powers of man asleep" with all its "anarchy and din, / Barbarian and infernal," its chattering monkeys, whirling children, grimacing and writhing buffoons, and its monstrosities—the "horse of Knowledge and the learned Pig," the "bust that speaks and moves its goggling eyes"—

All out-o'-the-way, far-fetched, perverted things,
All freaks of nature, all Promethean thoughts
Of Man, his dullness, madness, and their feats
All jumbled up together, to compose
A Parliament of Monsters.

This Parliament of Monsters is London to him, a fair or festival that mocks and derides the real nature of man, a distortion and perversion of his actual nobility (ll. 671–721).

So the book rises to an extraordinary pitch of indignation in the lines:

Oh, blank confusion! true epitome
Of what the mighty City in herself
To thousands upon thousands of her sons,
Living amid the same perpetual whirl
Of trivial objects . . .

(ll. 722–726.)

And it is recalled from this only by the vision of country scenes which are in explicit contrast, scenes which calm and exalt man everywhere and give him his insight into the unity of things, the "everlasting streams and woods," the sea propelling "from zone to zone, / Its currents," the "armies of clouds," the ancient hills and the "changeful language of their countenance" which "quickens the slumbering mind, and aids the thoughts / However multitudinous" to move with "order and relation" (ll. 741–761). This is change and variation, to be sure, but so orderly and harmonious as not to be change at all.

Book VIII opens with another kind of fair than Bartholomew Fair. Here the whole texture and movement of the verse changes, from the tumbling and pell-mell versification of Book VII to calm, even, slow lines describing how

> Long ere heat of noon,
> From byre or field the kine were brought; the sheep
> Are penned in cotes; the chaffering is begun.
> The heifer lows, uneasy at the voice
> Of a new master; bleat the flocks aloud.
> Booths are there none; a stall or two is here;
> A lame man or a blind, the one to beg,
> The other to make music; hither, too,
> From far, with basket, slung upon her arm,
> Of hawker's wares—books, pictures, combs, and pins—
> Some aged woman finds her way again,
> Year after year, a punctual visitant!
>
> (ll. 20–31.)

Here all's accustomed, ceremonious; and young and old are united in their innocent pleasures:

> The children now are rich, for the old today
> Are generous as the young; and, if content
> With looking on, some ancient wedded pair
> Sit in the shade together, while they gaze,
> 'A cheerful smile unbends the wrinkled brow,
> The days departed start again to life,
> And all the scenes of childhood reappear,
> Faint, but more tranquil, like the changing sun
> To him who slept at noon and wakes at eve.'
> Thus gaiety and cheerfulness prevail,
> Spreading from young to old, from old to young,
> And no one seems to want his share.
>
> (ll. 44–55.)

The whole scene is enclosed and as though protected by the ancient hills about them; and if, amid the magnificence of the hills, these people seem weak and little as infants, yet they are great also:

> For all things serve them: them the morning light
> Loves, as it glistens on the silent rocks;
> And them the silent rocks, which now from high
> Look down upon them; the reposing clouds;
> The wild brooks prattling from invisible haunts;
> And old Helvellyn, conscious of the stir
> Which animates this day their calm abode.
>
> (ll. 63–69.)

This is his vision of rural society, "rural peace," where

> the sun and sky,
> The elements and seasons as they change
> Do find a worthy fellow-labourer there . . .
>
> (ll. 101–103.)

These are the "common haunts of the green earth, / And ordinary interests of man," which refute the grotesqueries and illusions of London's dazzling press of the singular and deformed (ll. 116–117). This is the *real* world, he seems to be saying, and this the proper environment of man.

Everywhere he contrasts it with the false and merely mythological, not only with the city but also with the false paradises of exotic places and of romance. He says this tract was

> more exquisitely fair
> Than that famed paradise of ten thousand trees,
> Or Gehol's matchless gardens, for delight
> Of the Tartarian dynasty composed . . .
>
> (ll. 75–78.)

He says his first knowledge of the dignity of man came from the shepherds of his home country, who were distinctly not shepherds

> such as Saturn ruled 'mid Latian wilds,
> With arts and laws so tempered, that their lives
> Left, even to us toiling in this late day,
> A bright tradition of the golden age . . .
>
> (ll. 129–132.)

His shepherds were not those of Arcady or Arden, "nor such as Spenser fabled" (ll. 133–144). Those shepherds out of pastoral idylls and romances were indeed beautiful, and led beautiful lives, with their May games and garlands and "lighter graces" (ll. 144–156), but they led lives too luxuriant and easy to be meaningful to him. He seems almost unable to stop insisting that *his* shepherds are not of the golden age, and yet he seems nostalgic for that age, celebrating it again and again in rich lines. Germany, Goslar, had been such a golden place for him, he says, where the shepherd

> comes with spring-time, there abides
> All summer, and at sunrise ye may hear
> His flageolet, to liquid notes of love
> Attuned . . .
>
> (ll. 198–201.)

But in the end he rejects such pastoralism, with more regret though for the same reasons that he had rejected London—its unreality and lack of simplicity—and announces his faith in his own home country and its unluxuriant produce:

> Yet, hail to you
> Moors, mountains, headlands, and ye hollow vales,
> Ye long deep channels for the Atlantic's voice,
> Powers of my native region! Ye that seize
> The heart with firmer grasp! Your snows and streams
> Ungovernable, and your terrifying winds,
> That howl so dismally for him who treads
> Companionless your awful solitudes!
>
> (ll. 215–222.)

He describes with care the hard life of the shepherd of this country, the dangers and privations he undergoes, and the hard simplicity of his daily routine. This is a

> freeman, wedded to his life of hope
> And hazard, and hard labour interchanged
> With that majestic indolence so dear
> To native man.
>
> (ll. 253–256.)

This is man the "worthy fellow-labourer" of sun and sky, "man free, man working for himself, with choice / Of time and place, and object" (ll. 105–106).

But—and this is the main question before us—has he not substituted one kind of pastoralism, one kind of idealization and simplification, for another? For though he is at pains to describe the hard, harsh facts of this "native man's" environment and to contrast him to the shepherds of golden idylls, and though he is willing to admit theoretically that he is a "man with the most common" and suffers "with the rest / From vice and folly, wretchedness and fear" (ll. 288–291), he still contemplates him under an aspect of glory, and sees him crushing out "a livelier fragrance from the flowers of lowly thyme," leaping from crag to crag while the "lingering dews of morn / Smoke round him," and descending at last through a thick fog, "his sheep like Greenland bears." Stepping

> Beyond the boundary line of some hill-shadow,
> His form hath flashed upon me, glorified
> By the deep radiance of the setting sun.
>
> (ll. 238–270.)

The issue is not simple. Wordsworth certainly knew he had made an idealized image out of this shepherd and his "ordinary interests." But he was not always aware of the implications of making him so, and that this idealization had unexpected and sometimes distressing effects in his poetry.

He says man was thus "ennobled outwardly before my sight," and defiantly he says:

> Call ye these appearances—
> Which I beheld of shepherds in my youth,
> This sanctity of Nature given to man—
> A shadow, a delusion, ye who pore
> On the dead letter, miss the spirit of things,
> Whose truth is not a motion or a shape
> Instinct with vital functions, but a block
> Or waxen image which yourselves have made,
> And ye adore! But blessed be the God
> Of Nature and of Man that this was so;

That men before my inexperienced eyes
Did first present themselves thus purified,
Removed, and to a distance that was fit . . .

By first seeing man under this glorious aspect, he says:

I had my face turned toward the truth, began
With an advantage furnished by that kind
Of prepossession, without which the soul
Receives no knowledge that can bring forth good,
No genuine insight ever comes to her.
(ll. 293–327.)

And this is the noblest statement of his theme:

In the midst stood Man,
Outwardly, inwardly contemplated,
As, of all visible natures, crown, though born
Of dust, and kindred to the worm; a Being,
Both in perception and discernment, first
In every capability of rapture,
Through the divine effect of power and love;
As, more than anything we know, instinct
With godhead, and, by reason and by will,
Acknowledging dependency sublime.
(ll. 485–494.)

But it is with just such a statement, marvelous as it is, that we begin to cavil, for there is a real question whether he has not, in
seeing how man is instinct with godhead, forgotten his descent
from the dust and kinship with the worm, his involvement in
vice and folly, wretchedness and fear.

Book IV, "Summer Vacation," is a case in point. There Wordsworth tells how he came home from Cambridge, as though from
unreality to reality, full of joy at his return:

I overlooked the bed of Windermere,
Like a vast river, stretching in the sun.
With exultation, at my feet I saw
Lake, islands, promontories, gleaming bays,
A universe of Nature's fairest forms
Proudly revealed with instantaneous burst,
Magnificent, and beautiful, and gay.
(ll. 5–11.)

He ran shouting down the hill to greet the old ferryman, and visited eagerly all the scenes of his childhood. His coming home was like putting off the suit of clothes that had been Cambridge:

> Gently did my soul
> Put off her veil, and, self-transmuted, stood
> Naked, as in the presence of her God.
>
> (ll. 150–152.)

And, though he was not fully conscious of it, he communed with nature in the old way, responding to the way "life pervades the undecaying mind" and discovering once again how

> the immortal soul with God-like power
> Informs, creates, and thaws the deepest sleep
> That time can lay upon her . . .
>
> (ll. 165–168.)

Of course he was not unchanged. There was a new perception of the lives of the people around him, conditioned by his knowledge of how time had worked upon them:

> A freshness also found I at this time
> In human Life, the daily life of those
> Whose occupations really I loved;
> The peaceful scene oft filled me with surprise
> Changed like a garden in the heat of spring
> After an eight-days' absence. For (to omit
> The things which were the same and yet appeared
> Far otherwise) amid this rural solitude,
> A narrow Vale where each was known to all,
> 'Twas not indifferent to a youthful mind
> To mark some sheltering bower or sunny nook,
> Where an old man had used to sit alone,
> Now vacant; pale-faced babes whom I had left
> In arms, now rosy prattlers at the feet
> Of a pleased grandame tottering up and down;
> And growing girls whose beauty, filched away
> With all its pleasant promises, was gone
> To deck some slighted playmate's homely cheek.
>
> (ll. 191–208.)

His perceptions of nature too had more "human-heartedness" about them, were more aware of and compassionate toward the effects of time upon it:

> But now there opened on me other thoughts
> Of change, congratulation or regret,
> A pensive feeling! It spread far and wide;
> The trees, the mountains shared it, and the brooks . . .
>
> (ll. 231–242.)

He saw the mortal scene no longer as an angel might, but as a human being does.

And yet this is not the main tendency of the book, just as it is not the main tendency of the poem as a whole. We might think this new interest in his neighbors and "human-hearted" sympathy for nature, as a fellow victim of time, is evidence for what he means by the love of nature leading to the love of man. It is not. The tendency of this book is away from his time-ridden neighbors to a far more noble but in the end peculiar and special image of man. Wordsworth tells how one morning, after an all-night party with his friends, he left the "flower-decked room" and started home alone, over a road that

> glittered to the moon
> And bore the semblance of another stream
> Stealing with silent lapse to join the brook
> That murmured in the vale.

Everything was still, as though he were the only being alive in the world, when suddenly he saw "an uncouth shape," "of stature tall," "stiff, lank, and upright." A "more meagre man was never seen by night or day"; "long were his arms, pallid his hands; his mouth / Looked ghastly in the moonlight." He was evidently an old soldier, and he was alone, "and in his dress appeared / A desolation, a simplicity" to which the "trappings of a gaudy world" made a strange background. Wordsworth approached him and asked his history, and the veteran told his story with a "quiet uncomplaining voice." In all he said, "there was a strange half-absence" as of one "knowing too well the importance of his theme, / But feeling it no longer." Having listened to his story, Wordsworth took him to a nearby cottage and procured him lodging:

> In comfort, I entreated that henceforth
> He would not linger in the public ways,
> But ask for timely furtherance and help
> Such as his state required. At this reproof,
> With the same ghastly mildness in his look,
> He said, 'My trust is in the God of Heaven,
> And in the eye of him who passes me!'
>
> (ll. 370–460.)

What is the moral of this story? The poet has just left the ordinary social occasions of his life, and has met this ghostly old man and helped him. Perhaps the moral is in the kind deed (this is supported by the old man's "reviving interests" when he is given shelter). But when Wordsworth, who performed the kind act, tells the old man he should have asked for help, he is *reproved* by him. And we cannot escape the feeling that the old man, that "ghostly figure," had been sent into the poet's life as a kind of revelation, as the Leech-gatherer was sent.[1] His lack of feeling about his own experience, then, may be what should be learned from him. This is a figure as close to the border of death as possible, and as far as can be from involvement in "the ordinary interests of man." Yet he is an image of that mankind which the love of nature leads us to love.

The ambiguity—or confusion—may lie exactly in this: in Book VIII Wordsworth proclaims his love for the "common haunts of the green earth / And ordinary interests of mankind," but he also calls it "love for the human creature's absolute self" (ll. 116–123). The ideal shepherd stalking through the fog and the old man met on the solitary moonlit road are alternative images for that "absolute self," and they express in different ways the mankind to which Wordsworth's love of nature leads him. But they are idealized, though differently: they are abstractions, as far as possible from the ordinary interests of mankind. Wordsworth's criticism of romantic pastoral and his criticism of London and Cambridge, in terms of their unreality, is confusing for him as for the reader. He criticizes them because they do not represent the ordinary interests of man; yet the ordinary interests of man are for Wordsworth those which carry him furthest from the world of social experience, those which make him most alone and expressionless, those which strip him of his precious accidental involvements and emotional accouterments. The shepherd bounding across mountains is an heroic and attractive figure, and we are almost persuaded to accept him as an adequate abstract and summation of the capabilities of men, until we realize that he exists in another version, the pallid veteran on the lonely road.

This is a way of understanding how the marvelous naturalistic detail of Cambridge and London disturbs us, for it suggests a greater interest in experience than is actually true of this speaker, this poet. Just so, the apparent gain in "human-heartedness," described in Book IV, is really a sort of red herring, distracting Wordsworth at least, if not the reader. The whole tendency of the poem is in another direction, and there is no way we can call this boast of having found a "freshness" in human life a coherent irony. Wordsworth is fooling himself when he says so, and fooling us. The man his "nature" leads him to love is not so much a summation of human experience as he is an aberration from it.

In Book IX Wordsworth enters on his account of his disillusioning sojourn in France, and the issues of the poem begin to be framed in a narrower and more specific context. But they are the same issues. The dominant metaphors are of a sea journey, of being taken in by enchantment, and of the theater. France "lured" him forth (1. 34), and he "coasted round and round" the line of "Tavern, Brothel, Gaming-House, and Shop, / Great rendezvous of worst and best," the walk "of all who had a purpose, or had not" (ll. 53–56). As in London, his chief impression was of confusion and violence from which, as in London, he stood apart, a "hubbub wild" (1. 58) amid whose "concussions" he was "unconcerned,"

> Tranquil almost, and careless as a flower
> Glassed in a green-house, or a parlour shrub
> That spreads its leaves in unmolested peace,
> While every bush and tree, the country through,
> Is shaking to the roots . . .
>
> (ll. 86–91.)

The image is partly self-contemptuous, scornful that he should be so disengaged in the midst of great events. He was so because he brought to France—and to life in general—the attitude of a mere spectator, to whom the Revolution was nothing more than a stage play:

> I was unprepared
> With needful knowledge, had abruptly passed
> Into a theatre, whose stage was filled
> And busy with an action far advanced.
>
> (ll. 92–95.)

Of course this means that he was not *yet* involved as he would be involved later; but even later, as we shall see, this hubbub of experience into which he had thrust himself retained a kind of unreality, so that it could not actually touch him. This metaphor of the theater may in itself be saying that the Revolution was in fact no more than a stage play, an illusion, and we are reminded of how the metaphor applied to London and Cambridge. Reality for him was elsewhere. Just so, he may be saying that it is better to live in a greenhouse, to be protected and apart from the vicissitudes of the open air.

He spent some time among Royalist officers, and regarded them as blights in nature, saw in them signs of a dislocation of natural processes, so that at least in one instance their politics were reflected in the unnatural decay of the body:

> One, reckoning by years,
> Was in the prime of manhood, and erewhile
> He had sate lord in many tender hearts;
> Though heedless of such honours now, and changed:
> His temper was quite mastered by the times,
> And they had blighted him, had eaten away
> The beauty of his person, doing wrong
> Alike to body and to mind: his port,
> Which once had been erect and open, now
> Was stooping and contracted, and face,
> Endowed by Nature with her fairest gifts
> As much as any that was ever seen,
> A ravage out of season, made by thoughts
> Unhealthy and vexatious.
>
> (ll. 139–153.)

Yet this is not so simply because of his politics, with which Wordsworth disagreed. It is a more general commentary on the times.
This natural disturbance, disturbance in nature, could be seen in
anyone, without reference to party or beliefs:

> 'Twas in truth an hour
> Of universal ferment; mildest men
> Were agitated; and commotions, strife
> Of passion and opinion, filled the walls
> Of peaceful houses with unquiet sounds.
> The soil of common life was, at that time,
> Too hot to tread upon.
>
> (ll. 161–167.)

"The land all swarmed with passions, like a plain / Devoured
by locusts," and the great events of the day were like "earth-
quakes" (ll. 175–180). It was not the evil of one particular set of
opinions, but the "state of things," the passionate time itself, which
was to be in the poem significant as the symbol of the human condition, the unquiet mind of ordinary man.

Wordsworth visited with Royalists, but his sympathies could
not be with them, since he had been brought up in a region that
by nature took no account of artificial order or degree, a region
where all men were "brothers" "in honour, as in one community,"
and where this equality had been taught him by "God's mysterious power / Made manifest in Nature's sovereignty."

> It could not be
> But that one tutored thus should look with awe
> Upon the faculties of men, receive
> Gladly the highest promises, and hail,
> As best, the government of equal rights
> And individual worth.
>
> (ll. 215–243.)

Thus he was led "naturally," by the tutelage of nature, into his
political error, or rather into the error *of being political at all*, of
putting his faith in man's power to order his world successfully.
This is not all ironic, and one is hard put to say what proportion
of it *is* ironic. The ideal of political equality is always honored by

the poem; it is only later that the poem discovers how impossible
it is to realize such an ideal, the nature of man being what it is.
But surely there is some irony attached to his description of what
he was at this time, when he opposed the Royalists with a zeal that
"burst / Forth like a polar summer," an event in nature as "unnatural," as disturbing to the order and quiet of things, as a plague
or an earthquake (ll. 254–256). And surely this irony is made
more explicit when he says:

> their reason seemed
> Confusion-stricken by a higher power
> Than human understanding, their discourse
> Maimed, spiritless; and, in their weakness strong,
> I triumphed.
>
> (ll. 258–262.)

Not that the Royalists were right, but that he was wrong. His
ideal was perhaps better than theirs, attested to by nature. But he
was wrong to think it could ever be actual. He was, in his Republican allegiance, being led once again into a false paradise.

The rest of the book is concerned with Wordsworth's relationship with the noble Republican Beaupuy, and here the poet expresses the noblest political sympathies, and does so quite seriously,
quite sincerely, but treats them also with a tactful and beautiful
irony. The irony depends in part on the pattern of dominant
imagery which the poem has already established in our minds.
Beaupuy wandered through the events of that changeful time in
"perfect faith,"

> As through a book, an old romance, or tale
> Of Fairy, or some dream of actions wrought
> Behind the summer clouds.

Beaupuy loved man "as man," and together he and Wordsworth
looked forward to the great epoch of human love and peace which
would follow on the successful conclusion of the Revolution. They
spoke

> Of civil government, and its wisest forms;
> Of ancient loyalty, and chartered rights,
> Custom and habit, novelty and change . . .

They "added dearest themes" of

> Man and his noble nature, as it is
> The gift which God has placed within his power,
> His blind desires and steady faculties
> Capable of clear truth, the one to break
> Bondage, the other to build liberty
> On firm foundations, making social life,
> Through knowledge spreading and imperishable,
> As just in regulation, and as pure
> As individual in the wise and good.

They saw in the Revolution

> A living confirmation of the whole
> Before us, in a people from the depth
> Of shameful imbecility uprisen,
> Fresh as the morning star.

They saw

> in rudest men,
> Self-sacrifice the firmest; generous love,
> And continence of mind, and sense of right,
> Uppermost in the midst of fiercest strife.
>
> (ll. 288–388.)

The lines pay all honor to Beaupuy and to these conversations, yet they are finally ironic too, and look back on this period with the sweet and tender nostalgic admiration one gives to the follies of one's youth. The lines are the more ironic because sincere, for the time was essentially pastoral and romantic, when Wordsworth and Beaupuy walked together beside the Loire, talking of these things,

> Or in wide forests of continuous shade,
> Lofty and over-arched, with open space
> Beneath the trees, clear footing many a mile—
> A solemn region.

Appropriately, Wordsworth often "slipped in thought" into reveries of old romances, of Ariosto and Tasso and Spenser, for this idyll with Beaupuy was that kind of romance, with the same ideal beauty and—in Wordsworth's view—the same unreality. In their walks they came upon signs of Republican devastation—the ruins of a church, the signs of an old order that had been overthrown— and the signs were like warnings which Wordsworth did not yet heed more than faintly. When Beaupuy and Wordsworth chanced to meet "a hunger-bitten girl" who crept along "fitting her languid gait / Unto a heifer's motion," Beaupuy said, " 'Tis against *that* / That we are fighting," and Wordsworth was heartily in accord:

> I with him believed
> That a benignant spirit was abroad
> Which might not be withstood, that poverty
> Abject as this would in a little time
> Be found no more, that we should see the earth
> Unthwarted in her wish to recompense
> The meek, the lowly, patient child of toil.
>
> (ll. 431–532.)

The picture of the girl is extremely moving, and the way it compels us to take seriously the hopes of Wordsworth and Beaupuy is the condition of the irony's power—though how consciously the irony was thought of as such is always a question. In the context of the whole poem, the lines are critical of their naïveté in thinking things could ever be set right by political action, or indeed by any sort of human endeavor.

Book X opens with a description of the day Wordsworth left the vicinity of the Loire to return to Paris, and it describes the state of affairs in France on that day. Wordsworth knew that crimes had been committed in the name of the Revolution, but he was still sure that these "were past, / Earth free of them forever," that they were "ephemeral monsters, to be seen but once! / Things that could only show themselves and die" (ll. 46–47).

"Cheered with this hope," he returned to Paris, but almost immediately fell prey to his perceptions that all was *not* right; that as there had been violence before, so in the order of things among mankind, there would be violence again:

the fear gone by
Pressed on me almost like a fear to come.
I thought of those September massacres,
Divided from me by one little month,
Saw them and touched; the rest was conjured up
From tragic fictions or true history,
Remembrances and dim admonishments.
The horse is taught his manage, and no star
Of wildest course but treads back his own steps;
For the spent hurricane the air provides
As fierce a successor; the tide retreats
But to return out of its hiding-place
In the great deep; all things have second birth;
The earthquake is not satisfied at once . . .

He began to feel this necessity of tragedy and disaster in human affairs almost as a personal guilt and a nightmare of horror:

And in this way I wrought upon myself,
Until I seemed to hear a voice that cried,
To the whole city, 'Sleep no more.' The trance
Fled with the voice to which it had given birth;
But vainly comments of a calmer mind
Promised soft peace and sweet forgetfulness.
The place, all hushed and silent as it was,
Appeared unfit for the repose of night,
Defenceless as a wood where tigers roam.

(ll. 48–93.)

And this way of regarding things was not entirely characteristic of him at that time. It was but a warning of his final despair, for though he saw the violence that would ensue, and saw that France would not be able to resolve things alone, still he was optimistic about the result:

from all doubt
Or trepidation for the end of things
Far was I, far as angels are from guilt.

(ll. 143–145.)

The simile of angels reminds us of, may consciously allude to, the lines in Book IV which describe how, before he had learned to see the pathos in the time-ridden lives around him, he had loved "as a blessed spirit / Or Angel, if he were to dwell on earth" (ll. 236–238). He was as disengaged as an angel from the experience of mankind, and though his naïveté about the human condition was as beautiful as that of some angel about the earth, and as faithful to its vision of purity and changelessness, it was naïveté nevertheless.

He felt in himself an heroic desire and even a capacity to set things right, to take command and do all himself; and though this was wrong, naïve, and untrue to the facts of human experience, in which endeavor necessarily means defeat, the ideal of the nobility of the individual mind which inspired it was in another sense right:

> And, lastly, if the means on human will,
> Frail human will, dependent should betray
> Him who too boldly trusted them, I felt
> That 'mid the loud distractions of the world
> A sovereign voice subsists within the soul,
> Arbiter undisturbed of right and wrong,
> Of life and death, in majesty severe
> Enjoining, as may best promote the aims
> Of truth and justice, either sacrifice,
> From whatsoever region of our cares
> Or our infirm affections Nature pleads,
> Earnest and blind, against the stern decree.
>
> (ll. 178–190.)

Having this faith in individual purity and heroism, thinking that the virtue of "one paramount mind" (l. 211) could have solved everything, he was reluctant to return to England. But return he had to, to be shocked by England's taking arms against France. He felt himself uprooted from his old loyalties and forced to rejoice in England's defeats. Everywhere—in England, in France —he saw confusion, the judgment of the wise no better than the indiscretion of the foolish:

> Withal a season dangerous and wild,
> A time when sage Experience would have snatched
> Flowers out of any hedge-row to compose
> A chaplet in contempt of his grey locks.
>
> (ll. 311–314.)

France seemed like hell, and (reminding us again of Cambridge and London) like a giant mad festival, in which "domestic carnage now filled the whole year / With feast-days" (ll. 356–357), in which the worst crimes were committed in the name of Liberty. It was a

> woeful time for them whose hopes survived
> The shock; most woeful for those few who still
> Were flattered, and had trust in human kind . . .
> (ll. 386–388.)

Here the accent of despair is unmistakable, and the frame of reference of the whole poem unmistakably widened, so that his commentary applies to more than the political situation in France or England, to more than this troubled time alone, to the nature of mankind itself. It is more and more clear that these books about the French Revolution are a kind of metaphor for human involvements in general.

Wordsworth was still "flattered, and had trust in human kind," and hopes of a better future growing out of these times. Like an ancient prophet, he saw everywhere signs that a terrible retribution would overtake the criminals of the time; he foresaw that "wild blasts of music thus could find their way / Into the midst of turbulent events," so that "worse tempests might be listened to." He "clearly saw" that the terrible harvest was reaped not by popular government and equality, but by a

> terrific reservoir of guilt
> And ignorance filled up from age to age,
> That could no longer hold its loathsome charge,
> But burst and spread in deluge through the land.
> (ll. 437–480.)

This is not entirely ironic against himself. If he thought the guilt was historical—and certainly he did—then it is ironic, for the image suggests that once having burst, the reservoir of guilt would give way to a new era of hope, about which there could be valid expectations. But in another sense the guilt is definitively human, the necessary concomitant of the "troubled human heart"; and though retribution would come, it would not be political retribution necessarily, and would not be retribution against tyrants and criminals only, but against humanity in general.

Still Wordsworth did not really know this, and his failure to know it is the occasion for the most spectacular piece of irony in the poem. After his return to England, the poet went one day to visit the grave of his old teacher. The day was beautiful:

> Over the smooth sands
> Of Leven's ample estuary lay
> My journey, and beneath a genial sun,
> With distant prospect among gleams of sky
> And clouds, and intermingling mountain tops,
> In one inseparable glory clad,
> Creatures of one ethereal substance met
> In consistory, like a diadem
> Or crown of burning seraphs as they sit
> In the empyrean.

The elaboration and pomp of the lines is patently deliberate, for they are a sign of the self-delusion that still persisted in Wordsworth, like the delusive oriental palaces he had contrasted with his native region years before. The "pastoral vales" of his childhood "lay unseen" "underneath that pomp / Celestial," as if he had forgotten them. In his joy at the scene, he was made sad by being reminded of the grave he had visited that morning. But he was still unwarned by the example of Matthew, the old man we have heard despairing over the possibilities of human experience in this world.

There were other signs too that should have warned him, the remains of a "Romish chapel" now destroyed by time, and the "great sea" which "heaved at a safe distance, far retired," at low tide—he had forgotten what his nightmarish time in Paris ought to have taught him, that "the tide retreats / But to return out of its hiding-place in the great deep." The scene seemed merely "bright and cheerful" to him, and all he "saw or felt / Was gentleness and peace." So in spite of all these warnings that human experience is inevitably the victim of time and change, and that no human triumph can last, he heard with uncritical joy the news that Robespierre was dead:

Great was my transport, deep my gratitude
To everlasting Justice, by this fiat
Made manifest. 'Come now, ye golden time,'
Said I forth-pouring on those open sands
A hymn of triumph: 'as the morning comes
From out the bosom of the night, come ye:
Thus far our trust is verified . . .'

There is a terrific irony in his comparison of man's social experience to the morning coming out of night's bosom, for it is precisely *not* with this sort of order that human affairs proceed,
peacefully, acquiescently, without shock. It was his error to think
man too easily like nature, to take too optimistic a view of man's
fate:

Then schemes I framed more calmly, when and how
The madding factions might be tranquillised,
And how through hardships manifold and long
The glorious renovation would proceed.
Thus interrupted by uneasy bursts
Of exultation, I pursued my way
Along that very shore which I had skimmed
In former days, when—spurring from the Vale
Of Nightshade, and St. Mary's mouldering fane,
And the stone abbot, after circuit made
In wantonness of heart, a joyous band
Of school-boys hastening to their distant home
Along the margin of the moonlight sea—
We beat with thundering hoofs the level sand.

(ll. 514–603.)

The poem makes no explicit comment on its quotation of itself
here,[2] and almost needs none. As in childhood he had been almost deceived into thinking that the abbey existed out of time
and that he could enjoy there a kind of timeless paradise on earth,
so in young adulthood he was still capable of being fooled by
human events into thinking that one fortunate happening would
bring at last the "golden time" for which he longed.

Indeed, things *did* seem better after Robespierre's death.
Book XI opens with the statement that "authority . . . put on a
milder face," and "terror ceased," and Wordsworth's confidence
was "unimpaired." He was confounding one victory with another

"higher far,—/ Triumphs of unambitious peace at home, / And noiseless fortitude" (ll. 1–21).

Confined to England, far from the practical effects of the Revolution, he became still more theoretical, began to meditate with ardor "on the rule / And management of nations," and in commenting on this the poem draws together images of Cambridge, London, and France. It is clear that he was still involved in a romance, a false paradise, a dream, and under the spell of enchantment:

> Bliss was it in that dawn to be alive,
> But to be young was very Heaven! O times,
> In which the meager, stale, forbidding ways
> Of custom, law, and statute, took at once
> The attraction of a country in romance!
> When Reason seemed the most to assert her rights
> When most intent on making of herself
> A prime enchantress—to assist the work,
> Which then was going forward in her name!
> Not favoured spots alone, but the whole Earth,
> The beauty wore of promise—that which sets
> (As at some moments might not be unfelt
> Among the bowers of Paradise itself)
> The budding rose above the rose full blown.
> What temper at the prospect did not wake
> To happiness unthought of? The inert
> Were roused, and lively natures rapt away!
> They who had fed their childhood upon dreams,
> The play-fellows of fancy, who had made
> All powers of swiftness, subtilty, and strength
> Their ministers,—who in lordly wise had stirred
> Among the grandest objects of the sense,
> And dealt with whatsoever they found there
> As if they had within some lurking right
> To wield it;—they, too, who of gentle mood
> Had watched all gentle motions, and to these
> Had fitted their own thoughts, schemers more mild,
> And in the regions of their peaceful selves;—
> Now was it that *both* found, the meek and lofty
> Did both find helpers to their hearts' desire,
> And stuff at hand, plastic as they could wish,—
> Were called upon to exercise their skill,

> Not in Utopia,—subterranean fields,—
> Or some secreted island, heaven knows where!
> But in the very world, which is the world
> Of all of us,—the place where, in the end,
> We find our happiness, or not at all!

This world itself seemed to have become Utopia, and submissive in every way to the individual will:

> Why should I not confess that Earth was then
> To me, what an inheritance, new-fallen,
> Seems, when the first time visited, to one
> Who hither comes to find in it his home?
>
> (ll. 98–148.)

But when France turned oppressor and all things conspired to disillusion him, Wordsworth turned to "speculative schemes" that promised to "abstract the hopes of Man / Out of his feelings," to be fixed "for ever in a purer element." He turned to Godwinism, and gloried in a reason which could with "a resolute mastery" shake off "infirmities of nature, time, and place," and build "social upon personal Liberty" (ll. 223–240). The unsettling times had made him free to work upon his world as if he were free of its restrictions and limitations, and so he fared,

> Dragging all precepts, judgments, maxims, creeds,
> Like culprits to the bar; calling the mind,
> Suspiciously, to establish in plain day
> Her titles and her honours; now believing,
> Now disbelieving.

And the inevitable end of this false mastery of the world was of course perplexity and despair. He was

> endlessly perplexed
> With impulse, motive, right and wrong, the ground
> Of obligation, what the rule and whence
> The sanction; till, demanding formal *proof*,
> And seeking it in everything, I lost
> All feeling of conviction, and, in fine,
> Sick, wearied out with contrarieties,
> Yielded up moral questions in despair.
>
> (ll. 293–305.)

He was saved from this despair by his sister, who maintained
for him a "saving intercourse" with his "true self":

> for, though bedimmed and changed
> Much, as it seemed, I was no further changed
> Than as a clouded and a waning moon:
> She whispered still that brightness would return,
> She, in the midst of all, preserved me still
> A Poet, made me seek beneath that name,
> And that alone, my office upon earth;
> And lastly, as hereafter will be shown,
> If willing audience fail not, Nature's self,
> By all varieties of human love
> Assisted, led me back through opening day . . .
>
> (ll. 333–352.)

He was saved by her and by "Nature's self"—the syntax is ambiguous and the ambiguity significant. Dorothy was not so much
a person to him as the symbol of nature's power, instinctive and
unconscious in all her dealings with the natural scene, one with it.

This is the crisis of the poem and the resolution of the crisis,
the place to which everything has led. The hero is in his deepest
trouble, and this is the story of his rescue from that trouble. It
seems curiously hurried and perfunctory, somehow anticlimactic.

Nor is it surprising that this should be so, when we reflect that
the crisis was meaningless to his "true self." He had been, at worst,
"no further changed / Than as a clouded and a waning moon,"
and like the moon would inevitably get free of the clouds and
wax once more to his fullest brightness. His sister and her counsel
had not saved him from any real danger, for there had been no
real danger at all. She merely reminded him of his "true self," the
self which had been within him all along, remote from all his
experiences and indeed remote from experience itself, with the
exception of that mysterious communion with nature which he had
first felt in early childhood. The true self is inviolable and unchangeable. It proceeds according to its own laws, which are remarkably like cosmic and other nonhuman natural laws, as for
example the waxing and waning of the moon, the coming and going of clouds. It is, that is to say, totally undramatic in character,
has no crisis because it is immune to any danger, and is immune

from any danger because it is immune to any but metaphysical experiences. (Thus experience in time is symbolic in still another sense. It takes place so that the true self can discover its own nature. The rigors of experience are thus virtually ritualistic.)

There is a very large qualification to be made here. All this is true if we regard the poem as sacramentalist in doctrine, an account of how the poet learned to return to that orderly and harmonious nature from which he had never really been away. The order of nature had informed his mind in earliest childhood and had created in his consciousness powers which kept him safe from all dangers and at last brought him back to the fullest realization that he was a poet and that his proper function was therefore to record and symbolize the marvelous order in nature, so that at last all men should be brought to realize that they have similar powers in themselves. *The Prelude* is in this sense truly the story of the "Growth of a Poet's Mind," as its subtitle suggests. Our main effort so far has been to show how this growth, this passage through experience, has implications profoundly hostile to "ordinary" human experience and constitutes a withdrawal from the world which is profoundly disturbing. *The Prelude* is our summary example of how a symbolic or sacramentalist view of the world tends to derogate or at least limit the variety of "ordinary" human emotions and involvements, those defined by limitation in time and space. For a poet like Wordsworth, the world is not so much the scene of such involvements as it is a kind of cipher or hieroglyph, symbolizing man's fundamental and unchanging relation to order. Those things in man which must be defined as distinctively human can only be regarded as intrusions into, even perversions of, that fundamental relation.

But it is just here that something further must be said. When we examined the shorter poems of this period we discovered that there was still another element in the verse, destructive not only of the ordinary values of experience but of those of the sacramental view as well. We called this "the mystical yearning." It arises, perhaps, from Wordsworth's despair over the human personality, his recognition that, with all its accidentality, with all its distinctively human emotions and attachments, it will keep intruding between the metaphysical capability of the mind and the order that capability is designed to apprehend. The natural scene can be the equivalent of eternal, but man, because he has personality, is doomed to his temporal limitation:

> Should the whole frame of earth by inward throes
> Be wrenched, or fire come down from far to scorch
> Her pleasant habitations, and dry up
> Old Ocean, in his bed left singed and bare,
> Yet would the living Presence still subsist
> Victorious, and composure would ensue,
> And kindlings like the morning—presage sure
> Of day returning and of life revived.
> But all the meditations of mankind,
> Yea, all the adamantine holds of truth
> By reason built, or passion, which itself
> Is highest reason in a soul sublime;
> The consecrated works of Bard and Sage,
> Sensuous or intellectual, wrought by men,
> Twin labourers and heirs of the same hopes;
> Where would they be?
>
> (Bk. V, ll. 30–45.)

Because of this limitation, which makes one despair of even the greatest human achievements (indeed *especially* of them), man's sacramental imagination is necessarily a failure, and the poet harkens desperately back to the lost childhood, which had exhibited a "mystical" relation to eternity and which needed no intercessors. The poem never seeks to assert, it is true, that this mysticism can be regained. But the effects of its nostalgia are apparent everywhere, at worst in the unresolved ambiguity of the concluding books, straining as they do at a tone of triumph which is constantly being undercut, and at best in such a passage as the dream of the stone and the shell in Book V (ll. 50–140). There the poet recognizes most clearly the fundamental pessimism of his attitude toward human experience and toward poetry, and there, because of this recognition, his vision is genuinely tragic. The stone and shell, geometry and poetry, order and passions, must be buried, for they are at the mercy of the deluging sea. And the truest function of poetry is to prophesy "destruction to the children of the earth / By deluge, now at hand." The relation of man to eternity is not that of the perceiver of order to the order he perceives. It is that of the victim to the sea which will obliterate him. The waters of the deep are always gathering upon us.

The answer to all this is to *desire* obliteration, to merge and become one with the sea, the abyss, the inchoate, that which is below and behind even the symbolic capacities of the mind themselves. The answer is to desire those states of being which are symbolized in the poetry by the childlike and the inarticulate. From one point of view the mystical yearning is but the extreme of the sacramental or symbolist view: it has the same characteristic of a contempt for definitively human experience, the same allegiance to the eternal over against the temporal. But it is different from the sacramental attitude, and hostile to it, in its total rejection of mortal things, even of those things which perfectly demonstrate order.

The sacramental view is optimistic, then, though in a special and disturbing sense, about the possibilities of human experience in this temporal way; the mystical yearning is thoroughly pessimistic. And the last three books of *The Prelude* are a record of the tension between the two—not so much the tension as the unresolved ambiguity they create when expressed together. The poet is faced, upon the occasion of his return to nature, with two choices, and he chooses both. The "growth" of the poet's mind may be thought of as a withdrawal from the ordinary experience of mankind, the experience of cities and wars, into the quietude of nature and into a corresponding quietism on the poet's part. We might expect, therefore, that the concluding books of the poem would be a triumphant vindication of what this withdrawal into the contemplation of nature can do for the poet, as poet. (Indeed, Books XII and XIII are entitled, "Imagination and Taste, How Impaired and Restored.") At last, we might say, he accepted the natural scene as the source and repository of those images by which he symbolized his oneness both with the natural scene and with the eternity which lies behind it. But everywhere we find that this is not quite true, that the experiences described in these last books are curiously ambiguous and that they lead us finally to the conclusion that Wordsworth is, perhaps without knowing it, going much further. The sum of his experience may turn out to be not so much the vindication of the poet's imagination, which we have called sacramental, as the vindication of the lost mystical imagination, which is the enemy of poetry as of all distinctively human experience. The poet is ambiguously celebrating a view of nature which accepts its order, its comings and goings, the tranquillity of the nonhuman natural scene, and at the same time a view of nature which rejects the temporal in favor of the eternal and seen man's search as culminating in seas and mists, not in order but in oblivion.

III

AT THE VERY END of *The Prelude,* Wordsworth says proudly to Coleridge that "what we have loved, / Others will love, and we will teach them how." He says that he and Coleridge will "instruct them how the mind of man becomes / A thousand times more beautiful than the earth / On which he dwells," that it will be "in beauty exalted" "above this frame of things," "as it is itself / Of quality and fabric more divine" (Bk. XIV, ll. 444–454). This is his proudest boast: that his doctrine of nature can indeed teach men how to live better with one another, that his doctrine is in the end a humanist doctrine which can effectually be taught. His most impressive instance of what such teaching could be is the extended image of the order and "society" of nature which is described early in Book XII:

> Ye motions of delight, that haunt the sides
> Of the green hills; ye breezes and soft airs,
> Whose subtle intercourse with breathing flowers,
> Feelingly watched, might teach Man's haughty race
> How without injury to take, to give
> Without offence; ye who, as if to show
> The wondrous influence of power gently used,
> Bend the complying heads of lordly pines,
> And, with a touch, shift the stupendous clouds
> Through the whole compass of the sky; ye brooks,
> Muttering along the stones, a busy noise
> By day, a quiet sound in silent night;
> Ye waves, that out of the great deep steal forth
> In a calm hour to kiss the pebbly shore,
> Not mute, and then retire, fearing no storm;

And you, ye groves, whose ministry it is
To interpose the covert of your shades,
Even as a sleep, between the heart of man
And outward troubles, between man himself,
Not seldom, and his own uneasy heart:
Oh! that I had a music and a voice
Harmonious as your own, that I might tell
What ye have done for me. The morning shines,
Nor heedeth Man's perverseness; Spring returns,—
I saw the Spring return, and could rejoice,
In common with the children of her love,
Piping on boughs, or sporting on fresh fields,
Or boldly seeking pleasure nearer heaven
On wings that navigate cerulean skies.

                                        (ll. 9–37.)

Everything is in harmony and love with everything else, and this harmony and love is capable of teaching "Man's haughty race / How without injury to take, to give / Without offence." It is the ministry of the groves to make man at peace with everything outside himself and with his own heart too.

Yet nothing is more characteristic of this imagination and of its greatest poem than that its celebration of nature as a humanistic agency, the friend and teacher of man, is accompanied by the most pessimistic doubts about man's capacity to learn. "The morning shines," he says, "Nor heedeth Man's perverseness." We have seen evidence upon evidence to suggest that this perverseness, man's positive capacity for disharmony, disunity, uneasiness, is indigenous to him and definitive of what he is. The waves kissing the shore are an instance of love which ought to set an example for man, but man is by definition haughty and his every effort to make a sweet and loving society is by definition but a pastoral dream, doomed to failure and disappointment. Only Wordsworth himself, since he had his lucky childhood and has his exemplary Dorothy, might succeed.

Yet his success, as we have seen, is not to enter into a fuller and sweeter communication with mankind generally. It is to retreat from humanity, to become as nearly as possible a natural and not a human thing. The very opening of this book is like a sigh of relief at escaping from the concerns of men:

> Long time have human ignorance and guilt
> Detained us, on what spectacles of woe
> Compelled to look, and inwardly oppressed
> With sorrow, disappointment, vexing thoughts,
> Confusion of the judgment, zeal decayed,
> And, lastly, utter loss of hope itself
> And things to hope for!
>
> (ll. 1–7.)

Wordsworth has come home to his proper attitudes, of which
Dorothy is the exemplar, the attitudes from which he had been
wrenched away (or thought he had) during his adventures among
men. But he cannot convince us that these attitudes are capable
of being taught, nor that he himself had really learned them
through an intelligible process of growth. This passage suggests
that the shape of the poem is finally circular, that the solution
to the problems it presents lies at last in a very simple return to
the childhood oneness with things and in a very simple rejection
of the concerns of men—"Not with these began / Our song, and
not with these our song must end." (ll. 7–8).

If Wordsworth had kept his harmony with things, he had
kept it through some magic which had preserved him as more a
natural than a human being, impervious to the assaults of his experience:

> So neither were complacency, nor peace,
> Nor tender yearnings, wanting for my good
> Through these distracted times; in Nature still
> Glorying, I found a counterpoise in her,
> Which, when the spirit of evil reached its height,
> Maintained for me a secret happiness.
>
> (ll. 38–43.)

Secret it was indeed, and it had to remain so. For most men there
was no Dorothy, nor any such harmonious childhood to which one
could magically return. Dorothy was, by her "benign simplicity of
life, / And through a perfect happiness of soul," perfectly "attuned" to nature, as lambs and birds, flowers and trees, are attuned, and as he himself had once been attuned (ll. 151–173).
And at last, so he declares, he learned to come back:

I had known
Too forcibly, too early in my life,
Visitings of imaginative power
For this to last: I shook the habit off
Entirely and for ever, and again
In Nature's presence stood, as now I stand,
A sensitive being, a *creative* soul.

(ll. 201–207.)

If this were all, if Wordsworth were clearly and simply celebrating his fortunate return to the oneness of nature, we would
still be troubled, since return involves nothing less than the rejection of what man has to be, with all his perverseness and his
definitively uneasy heart. But it is not all. In the very effort of
telling us that there are such resources in all our childhoods,
capable of lifting us up when fallen, Wordsworth expresses his
most profoundly melancholy lament for the failure of those resources in his own life. "There are in our existence spots of time,"
he says, "That with distinct pre-eminence retain / A renovating
virtue." Such moments are "scattered everywhere, taking their
date / From our first childhood." His example of these is a time
when as a child he went riding one day on the moors and became
separated from the servant who accompanied him. He came to a
terrifying and mysterious place, where a murderer had once been
hanged, the gibbet long since moldered away and only an inscrip-
tion in the ground remaining to tell what had happened. He fled
from the place in terror and, "reascending the bare common," saw

A naked pool that lay beneath the hills,
The beacon on the summit, and more near,
A girl, who bore a pitcher on her head,
And seemed with difficult steps to force her way
Against the blowing wind. It was, in truth,
An ordinary sight; but I should need
Colours and words that are unknown to man,
To paint the visionary dreariness
Which, while I looked all round for my lost guide,
Invested moorland waste and naked pool,
The beacon crowning the lone eminence,
The female and her garments vexed and tossed
By the strong wind.

(ll. 208–261.)

This is our strongest Wordsworth, the quintessence of his best style and sensibility. He found the record of some old human violence, the legend of it piously preserved by generations, as if man should always keep before him the knowledge of his own perversity. He fled from the place, but not to an easy refuge. Rather than lambs in the green field or birds in the bower, he found a naked pool, a melancholy beacon, and a girl at odds with the wind. Nothing is more dreary than this scene, yet it becomes for him the source of joy and strength. In memory there falls upon it a "spirit of pleasure" (l. 266), and not by any simple transforming energy of the memory at all, but from the union of the memory with a power that had been in the scene itself. The girl is in no facile harmony with the wind, but the vexing and tossing of her garments is as appropriate to it as the blowing of the wind against her is appropriate to what she is. She and the wind, taken together, are a symbol of the harmony that is in nature even when it seems most unharmonious. The symbol is powerfully expressive of man's predicament in time, which can produce murderers and murderous hearts, and at the same time symbolic of the solution to that predicament, which is the perception of harmony. Here it is as if the hero poet has gone boldly into the place where nature is least hospitable, most violent, and tamed it by discovering its unity. Disharmony is but a wrong way of seeing. Seen rightly, all vexation is peace, all feelings are one feeling. Beauty and fear, melancholy and joy, are one thing after all.

All this is immensely persuasive, since it founds our oneness with nature and with our childhoods on something that lies deeper than the superficies of our various emotions. The poet triumphantly finds his blessing not in some sunny bower but in visionary dreariness. But it is characteristic and significant that this victorious celebration of our integrity with our pasts and of the sources of our strengths turns elegiac; and does so in the cry of victory itself:

> Oh! mystery of man, from what a depth
> Proceed thy honours. I am lost, but see
> In simple childhood something of the base
> On which thy greatness stands; but this I feel,

That from thyself it comes, that thou must give,
Else never canst receive. The days gone by
Return upon me almost from the dawn
Of life . . .

If we forgot the doubts the rest of the poem has raised in us, if
we understood it only sacramentally and as a great statement of
the possibilities for man in nature, providing he will but coura-
geously find the harmony in elemental violence and dreariness,
the passage might end here, in undoubting and honorable self-
congratulation. But the passage itself expresses the doubt:

The days gone by
Return upon me almost from the dawn
Of life: the hiding-places of man's power
Open; I would approach them but they close.
I see by glimpses now; when age comes on,
May scarcely see at all . . .

(ll. 272–286.)

What has preceded this is Wordsworth's great expression of the
possibilities in nature of its redeeming powers for man; and this
is the great contradiction of those possibilities. It is for me one of
the most terrible instants in all his poetry, the admission of defeat
at the point of victory. To grow up and grow old is to grow away
from the secret sources of one's strength (which can only be understood as one's capacity for union with the eternal), and nothing—neither the poetic imagination which searches the landscape
for signs of its harmony and love, nor the mystical yearning for
an immediate oneness—can prevent that separation. For once the
poetry seems to know this itself and to know it plainly. For once
its self-knowledge is to be seen directly, not merely clinging to
the edges of the implications of his symbols.

This self-knowledge is not sustained. The poem cannot for
long contemplate its hero in this attitude of dignified self-pity,
seeing the sources of his power but seeing them as more and more
unattainable. He looks back to them, and they open as if to receive
him. He approaches them, and they close. It is as if he were lost
in the desert and always seeing before him an inviting mirage,
which promises rest and water but which always vanishes just as

he is about to reach it. How could such a mind sustain the plain knowledge of the absoluteness of its defeat?

Rather, the rhythm of these concluding books, which is the normal rhythm of Wordsworth's imagination itself, is a constant shifting between these attitudes, between the assertion that the harmony of nature is still possible and the knowledge that he (like all men) is by his very involvement in time cut off from such harmony. As in the great *Ode*, as in *Tintern Abbey*, the accent of hope and joy is countered everywhere by the accent of hopelessness.

Book XIII is more discursive than Book XII, and the verse is on the whole less distinguished. Its conflicting attitudes are presented more or less separately and piecemeal, not pressed out together through concrete instances. It opens with a simple theoretical statement, quite beautiful and quite misleading:

> From Nature doth emotion come, and moods
> Of calmness equally are Nature's gift:
> This is her glory; these two attributes
> Are sister horns that constitute her strength.
> Hence Genius, born to thrive by interchange
> Of peace and excitation, finds in her
> His best and purest friend; from her receives
> That energy by which he seeks the truth,
> From her that happy stillness of the mind
> Which fits him to receive it when unsought.
>
> (ll. 1–10.)

Nature, the "visible quality and shape / And image of right reason," is the mighty exemplar of the temperate life, gives birth to "no impatient or fallacious hopes, / No heat of passion or excessive zeal, / No vain conceits." It "trains / To meekness, and exalts by humble faith" and

> Holds up before the mind intoxicate
> With present objects, and the busy dance
> Of things that pass away, a temperate show
> Of objects that endure . . .

And what is true of this nature can be true of man and his "frame of social life" too:

Whate'er there is desirable and good
Of kindred permanence, unchanged in form
And function, or, through strict vicissitude
Of life and death, revolving.

(ll. 20–39.)

We are told that one can learn from nature how to look on nature
and man under the aspect of eternity, and find what is meaningful
in our experience without rejecting it out of hand. This view
allows the poet, so he claims, to find in man once more an "object
of delight, / Of pure imagination, and of love" (ll. 49–50), and
to fix his attention on great truths without being distracted by little
ones. This object of delight can be found, he declares, only among
simple and humble men, not among those who "thrust themselves
upon the passive world / As Rulers of the world," and such pure
and humble men exist among the "natural abodes of men, / Fields
with their rural works" and the "lonely roads," which are en-
riched with "human kindnesses and simple joys" (ll. 64–119).
This is the Wordsworthian pastoral again, and it is characteristic
that though it outlines an idyllic society in which all men communicate adequately with one another, "expressing liveliest
thoughts in lively words / As native passion dictates" (ll. 264–
265), and though it seems on the most obvious level to be a
perfectly unexceptionable celebration of ordinary humility and
gentleness, its tendency is to derogate and call into question the
arts of civilization themselves, "the courteous usages refined by
art," the books that "mislead us" and all the outward marks
"whereby society has parted man / From man" and made him
neglect "the universal heart" (ll. 186–220). And it is characteristic also that though the poem celebrates the articulation, the
communication possible in his ideal society, it celebrates above
everything else that which is so immediately in contact with truth
that it must remain mute:

Others, too,
There are among the walks of homely life
Still higher, men for contemplation framed,
Shy and unpractised in the strife of phrase;
Meek men, whose very souls perhaps would sink
Beneath them, summoned to such intercourse;

> Theirs is the language of the heavens, the power,
> The thought, the image, and the silent joy:
> Words are but under-agents in their souls;
> When they are, grasping with their greatest strength,
> They do not breathe among them: this I speak
> In gratitude to God, who feeds our hearts
> For his own service; knoweth, loveth us,
> When we are unregarded by the world.
>
> (ll. 265–278.)

The characteristic paradox of this pastoralism: the very thing which looks like incapacity to the eye of the ordinary world turns out to be the greatest capacity of all. Just as the intellectual eye is able to operate only when it has rejected the ministration of the bodily eye, or as the animal appetites and daily wants of men are obstructions which must be surmounted before true virtue and dignity are possible, so it is only when the language of men— the chief sign of their community together—is rejected that the language of the heavens can speak clearly to them. It is only when men are least men that they are most man.

At this point Wordsworth recalls still another event from his childhood, a time when, wandering on the plain, he saw the present scene vanish and

> Time with his retinue of ages fled
> Backwards, nor checked his flight until I saw
> Our dim ancestral Past in vision clear;
> Saw multitudes of men, and, here and there,
> A single Briton clothed in wolf-skin vest,
> With shield and stone-axe, stride across the wold;
> The voice of spears was heard, the rattling spear
> Shaken by arms of mighty bone, in strength,
> Long mouldered, of barbaric majesty.
>
> (ll. 318–326.)

He was given an insight into a past before history, as it were, and into a "society" so crude as hardly to be a society at all, and the very rudeness of his vision seems more appropriate to his rejection of men than the idyllic humble and rustic life he had been describing.

Surely it is not necessary at this point to recapitulate our earlier arguments about the shorter poems in this regard. *The Prelude* shows everywhere in these last books the same tendency to go beyond the sacramental view, with its acceptance of the orderly in nature, to a vision of the pure past, the pure childhood, the languageless and inexpressible, which amounts not to a use of the natural scene but to an obliteration of it.

But all this conflict which we find expressing itself in various ways through Books XII and XIII is best illustrated by examining the last important event and image in the poem, the ascent of Mount Snowdon, which is described at the beginning of the last book. Book XII opens with a passage describing the harmonious and courteous processes of natural things, the bowing of the pines, the advancing and retreating of the waves. This is the sacramental nature. Book XIV opens with an image far more ambiguous, far less plainly an image of order, far more plainly an image of mystery. The two images stand opposed to one another as summary emblems of the contest that always rages in this imagination, not only in *The Prelude* but in all the poems of the major period. The poet was to have learned how to reunite himself harmoniously with harmonious nature, but his journey ends with a vision of the formless sea, and among mists, and with the roaring waters of the abyss sounding in his ears.

He climbed Mount Snowdon in the company of others, but when the experience began to be really meaningful for him, when the moon suddenly shone forth, he forgot about the others and was, for all practical purposes, alone with its meaning. And its meaning is ambiguously a symbol of the sacramental and of the mystical imaginations. It is the vision of a scene where human life is unimaginable, all sea and torrent and mist, punctuated only by the backs of a hundred hills

> All over this still ocean; and beyond,
> Far, far beyond, the solid vapours stretched,
> In headlands, tongues, and promontory shapes,
> Into the main Atlantic, that appeared
> To dwindle, and give up his majesty,
> Usurped upon far as the sight could reach.

The sky, with its brilliant moon, its clarity, is suggestive here of the divine nature itself, that which is beyond both humanity and the ordinary natural scene, untroubled in its objective reality. The sky appears to dominate the world, and the moon—as indeed it does—controls the "billowy ocean," gazing down on it with sovereign pride as the ocean lies "all meek and silent." A beautiful and predictable symbol of the powers of the imagination or of that divine Power which is the source of all imaginations, controlling and ordering the visible world. And yet the poet hears about him the roaring of waterfalls:

> through a rift—
> Not distant from the shore whereon we stood,
> A fixed, abysmal, gloomy, breathing-place—
> Mounted the roar of waters, torrents, streams
> Innumerable, roaring with one voice;
> Heard over earth and sea, and, in that hour,
> For so it seemed, felt by the starry heavens.
>
> (ll. 11–62.)

It is power against power—the power of the clarifying moon, which not only discovers but even creates the order of natural things, over against the power of the abyss, that nature whose name is not order and harmony but chaos and mystery. If Wordsworth looked above and beyond himself, he saw the ordering moon; but he heard in his ears the inchoate and terrific sound of roaring waters.

What he had seen seemed to Wordsworth the "type of a majestic intellect," and therein he beheld the

> emblem of a mind
> That feeds upon infinity, that broods
> Over the deep abyss, intent to hear
> Its voices issuing forth to silent light
> In one continuous stream; a mind sustained
> By recognitions of transcendent power,
> In sense conducting to ideal form,
> In soul of more than mortal privilege.
>
> (ll. 70–77.)

And he goes on to say that this is the "very spirit" "higher minds" bring with them to deal with "the whole compass of the universe," so that they can be exalted both by the "enduring and the tran-

sient" in nature and can "build up greatest things / From least
suggestions" (ll. 86–102). This again is sacramental, a celebration
of the way the symbolic, the poetic imagination can use "every
image" and "every thought" to raise themselves "from earth
to heaven, from human to divine" (ll. 112–118). But the abstract explanation of the image is more orderly than the image
itself, and makes an insufficient account of the mists and of the
abyss of roaring waters. These appurtenances of the image suggest something other than building up greatest things from least
suggestions. They are a symbol of the mystery in man and nature,
the two mysteries which can only be joined by the mystical act;
and the possibility of the mystical act is bygone. The poet says
a little later that

> we have traced the stream
> From the blind cavern whence is faintly heard
> Its natal murmur; followed it to light
> And open day; accompanied its course
> Among the ways of Nature, for a time
> Lost sight of it bewildered and engulphed:
> Then given it greeting as it rose once more
> In strength, reflecting from its placid breast
> The works of man and face of human life . . .
>
> (ll. 194–202.)

But the place he comes to in the end is far from placid. It is roaring, abysmal, gloomy; and the image reflects the poet's own confusion about what he had come to.

He has returned to nature, but he cannot tell whether it is the
eternal nature as exhibited through the articulate processes of the
natural scene or the pure mystery of things which is not to be
distinguished from self-obliteration, or would not be if he could
truly return to that nature, really plunge himself into the abyss
and pass the limits of mortality. He cannot do so; he can only
yearn for it from the top of Mount Snowdon, remembering that
he had once been one with the things of nature and had required
no symbols. Not clarity but mists attend his vision.

Conclusion

THERE IS little more to say. Our main argument has been repeated time and again in tracing through these poems, and to repeat it once more, abstractly and summarily, would be merely tedious. The main contours of my view of Wordsworth's major poetry should be sufficiently clear by now.

Obviously one could write another book about the poetry which followed the great period, and just as obviously, it is no part of my plan to go into that subject. It seems plain to me that the poetry after about 1805 is generally quite inferior to the poetry written before that time. There are a number of very beautiful poems, enough certainly to have made Wordsworth an impressive poet even if he had not had his greatest years. But for the most part there is a shocking debilitation in his work. The symptoms of it are plain too: a flat and moralistic and not often very passionate adaptation of Christian and classical vocabularies; a tendency to increased garrulity; a soberly cheery optimism about the relations of man and nature, man and God, combined with a sort of peevishness against railroads and a zeal for capital punishment.

I would only ask one or two questions. Is it surprising—given the force of the yearning I have called "mystical" and the pessimism about its fulfillment—is it surprising that the poet should at last turn to other interests and other attitudes—in which, however, he could not fully or enthusiastically participate? He says a "deep distress" "humanized" his soul,[1] and is this not at once a kind of confession that the love of nature had not led to the love of man, and the declaration of a new aim and new interest which his imagination was not equipped to sustain? It sustains it, to be sure, in passage after passage of the late poetry which has to do with human death, for this remained for Wordsworth what it had always been, the most poignant of human experiences. But the imagination—Wordsworth's imagination—could by no means attach itself to human life in other ways nor detach itself from its old interests; and its old interests, whether he knew it consciously or not, had failed. His genius was his enmity to man, which he mistook for love, and his mistake led him into confusions which he could not bear. But when he banished the confusions, he banished his distinctive greatness as well.

Notes

CHAPTER ONE

Some Characteristics of Wordsworth's Style

[1] "Preface to . . . Lyrical Ballads," *The Poetical Works of William Wordsworth*, ed. E. de Selincourt and H. Darbishire, 5 vols. (London, 1940–1952), II, 394–395.

[2] *Biographia Literaria*, ed. J. Shawcross, 2 vols. (London, 1907), II, 109–111.

[3] *Poetical Works*, II, 393.

[4] Baruch Spinoza, *Selections*, ed. John Wild (New York, 1930), p. 383.

[5] The same, p. 387.

[6] The same, p. 387.

[7] *Biographia Literaria*, II, 109.

CHAPTER TWO

The Love of Nature

[1] *Poetical Works*, II, 174–176.

[2] The same, II, 211–212.

[3] "The Statesman's Manual," *Works*, ed. H. N. Coleridge and others, 17 vols. (London, 1839–1850), I, 250.

[4] The same, Appendix B, *Works*, I, 267.

[5] The same, Appendix B, *Works*, I, 269.

[6] The same, Appendix B, *Works*, I, 273.

[7] S. T. Coleridge, "On Poesy and Art," appended to *Biographia Literaria*, II, 253–257.

[8] "The Statesman's Manual," Appendix B, *Works*, I, 282.

[9] "On Poesy and Art," *Biographia Literaria*, II, 262.

[10] Alexander Pope, *An Essay on Man*, Epistle I, ll. 281–284.

[11] *Poetical Works*, IV, 279–285.

[12] *Biographia Literaria*, II, 111–113.

[13] I. A. Richards, *Coleridge on Imagination*, 2nd ed. (London, 1950), pp. 135–136.

[14] Quoted in *Poetical Works*, IV, 463–464. One of the notes dictated to Miss Fenwick in 1843.

[15] Lionel Trilling, *The Liberal Imagination* (New York, 1951), p. 151.

[16] The same, pp. 147–148.

[17] The same, p. 148.

[18] The same, p. 152.

CHAPTER THREE

The Love of Man

[1] Quoted in *Poetical Works*, IV, 415. From one of the notes dictated to Miss Fenwick in 1843.

[2] See "Resolution and Independence," *Poetical Works*, II, 235 (l. 5).

[3] See *The Prelude*, ed. E. de Selincourt (London, 1928), p. 425 (Bk. XII, ll. 31–32).

[4] *Poetical Works*, IV, 71–73.

[5] The same, IV, 69–71.

[6] The same, II, 80–94.

[7] The same, II, 47–50.

[8] The same, II, 227–235.

[9] *The Liberal Imagination*, pp. 147–148.

[10] *Poetical Works*, I, 236–238.

[11] The same, I, 234–236.

[12] Quoted in *Poetical Works*, I, 360. One of the notes dictated to Miss Fenwick in 1843.

[13] Quoted in *Poetical Works*, II, 440, n. 2.

[14] *The Rambler*, ed. S. C. Roberts (London, Everyman's Library, 1953), p. 78.

[15] The same, p. 90.

[16] *Some Versions of Pastoral* (Norfolk, Connecticut, n.d.), p. 15.

[17] Quoted in *Poetical Works*, II, 386–387.

[18] See Chapters XVII and XVIII, *passim*, of *Biographia Literaria*, II, 28–68. I am not, of course, referring to any *particular* question here, but to the general tenor of Coleridge's argument, which challenges, as I do, the meaning of Wordsworth's term "real," as in "the language really used by men."

[19] *Poetical Works*, II, 67–80.

[20] *The Early Letters of William and Dorothy Wordsworth,* ed. E. de Selincourt (Oxford, 1935), p. 297.

[21] Quoted in *Poetical Works,* II, 511–512. One of the notes dictated to Miss Fenwick in 1843.

[22] In the Preface, see especially *Poetical Works,* II, 435–444. In *The Prelude,* see especially Books XII–XIV, *passim.*

[23] See *Poetical Works,* II, 442.

[24] The same, II, 259–263.

CHAPTER FOUR

The Prelude

[1] See "Resolution and Independence," *Poetical Works,* II, 235–240.

[2] *The Prelude,* pp. 47–49 (Bk. II, ll. 128–137). The point of the allusion is even more complex than I have suggested: he is returning now to childhood and to the natural scene which will bring him peace.

Conclusion

[1] "Elegiac Stanzas Suggested by a Picture of Peele Castle," *Poetical Works,* IV, 259.

Index

The Limits of Mortality

has been composed in Linotype Caslon Old Face
and printed letterpress by Quinn & Boden Company, Inc.,
of Rahway, New Jersey

Wesleyan University Press
MIDDLETOWN, CONNECTICUT